M000013390

# Stadium Stories:

# Florida State Seminoles

### Gary Long

INSIDERS' GUIDE®

GUILFORD, CONNECTICUT
AN IMPRINT OF THE GLOBE PEQUOT PRESS

To buy books in quantity for corporate use
or incentives, call **(800) 962–0973, ext. 4551,**
or e-mail **premiums@GlobePequot.com.**

# INSIDERS' GUIDE®

Copyright © 2006 by Morris Book Publishing, LLC

All rights reserved. No part of this book may be reproduced or transmitted in any form by any means, electronic or mechanical, including photocopying and recording, or by any information storage and retrieval system, except as may be expressly permitted by the 1976 Copyright Act or by the publisher. Requests for permission should be made in writing to The Globe Pequot Press, P.O. Box 480, Guilford, Connecticut 06437.

Insiders' Guide is a registered trademark of Morris Book Publishing, LLC.
Stadium Stories is a trademark of Morris Book Publishing, LLC.

Text design: Casey Shain
All photos are courtesy of the Florida State University Sports Information Department.
Cover photos: *front cover:* Chris Weinke; *back cover:* top, Bobby Bowden; bottom, Chief Osceola.

Library of Congress Cataloging-in-Publication Data

Long, Gary (Gary L.)
    Stadium stories : Florida State Seminoles / Gary Long. — 1st ed.
        p. cm. — (Stadium stories series)
    ISBN-13: 978-0-7627-4093-2
    ISBN-10: 0-7627-4093-0
    1. Florida State University—Football—History. 2. Florida State Seminoles (Football team)—History. I. Title. II. Series.
GV958.F56L65 2006
796.332'630975988—dc22                                    2006041816

Manufactured in the United States of America
First Edition/First Printing

In memory of my loving parents, Bud and Jane, who gave
me life more than sixty-five years ago,
and for Evelyn, who helps keep it so invigorating and
enjoyable today.

# Acknowledgments

**I would like to thank** Florida State University sports information director Rob Wilson and assistants Jeff Purinton and Tina Thomas, as well as former SID Wayne Hogan, not only for their input for this book but also for their assistance throughout the time I covered the Seminoles.

Thanks to FSU coach Bobby Bowden and members of his staff over those twenty consecutive seasons, with special mention of defensive coordinator Mickey Andrews and Bowden's longtime secretary, Sue Hall.

Thanks to good friend Ted Findlay, who worked for me (sort of) in the U.S. Army's Fort Gordon (Georgia) public information office in 1963 and later paved my path to the *Miami Herald*.

Thanks to friend and colleague Bill Vilona and my sportswriting nephew, Dustin Long, for reading a couple chapters in their early form and providing valued opinion.

Thanks to Mike Urban and his wife, Ellen, for their encouragement and editing.

But mostly, thanks to the hundreds upon hundreds of players, from Heisman Trophy and Thorpe Award winners to walk-ons and reserves, who made writing about FSU football such a pleasure for so long.

# Contents

# Introduction

**Wide receiver Ronald Lewis,** approaching his 1989 senior season, sat in the atrium of Florida State's Moore Athletic Center and chatted with sportswriters on an August afternoon as incoming freshman Terrell Buckley strolled past toward the training room. One reporter popped up and asked, "Terrell, do you have a moment?" Though polite, Buckley said he was in a hurry and didn't have time to talk.

Lewis interrupted. "Hey, rookie, you've got time," the senior chided. Buckley, one of the more affable and loquacious players ever to wear garnet and gold, did an about-face, sat down with the writer, and answered his questions.

What the episode reflects is the level of cooperation and accessibility that flowed from the top down—from Coach Bobby Bowden through assistant coaches and players—and helped working-stiff beat reporters do their job. Older players quickly set the example for the younger ones. What made the task that much more enjoyable is that FSU football mattered.

For fourteen consecutive seasons, from 1987 through 2000, any discussion of college football's national championship necessarily included the Seminoles. They ascended the throne in 1993 and 1999 and arguably came within one victory of the title in a half-dozen seasons more.

So rare was defeat that FSU losses became more newsworthy than FSU victories. I covered the Miami Dolphins beat from 1976 through 1978, and I'll always remember the late Gene Miller, a two-time Pulitzer Prize winner, smiling at me as we passed in a hallway and saying, "Isn't it great to be read!"

In South Florida you can't write enough about the Dolphins to satisfy voracious appetites for information. And Florida State's successes made their exploits and the rare failure "must" reading for any avid college football fan for those fourteen seasons.

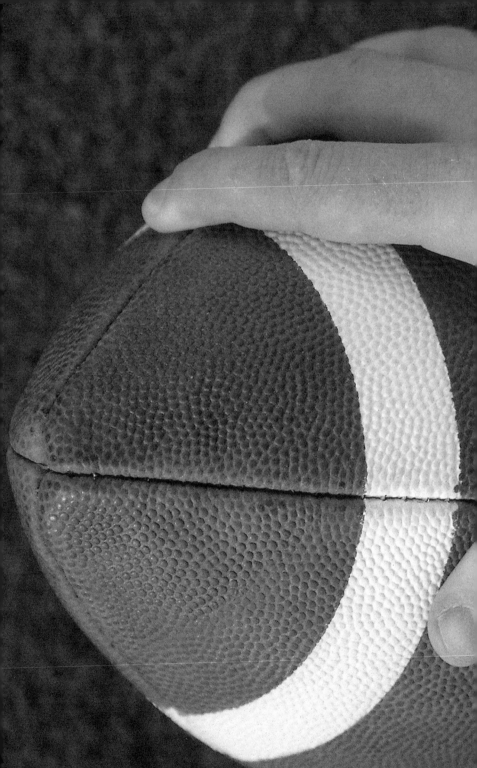

# Perfection

Peter Warrick trotted into the huddle supremely confident that he could supply an exclamation point not only to one of the most pyrotechnic displays of offense in a national championship game but to an era of sustained excellence unmatched in college football history. "I asked the offensive line[men], 'What do y'all want me to do? Y'all want me to finish 'em?'" Warrick related animatedly in the euphoric aftermath of what is arguably Florida State University's greatest victory. "They said, 'Finish 'em, Pete.'" And Warrick did.

The superstar All-American made one of the most sensational catches of a spectacular career to seal FSU's 46–29 Sugar Bowl conquest of Virginia Tech. It was also the climax to the one perfect season in a fourteen-year assault on the record books engineered by Bobby Bowden, the folksy Alabama native who has become a coaching icon.

Bowden, seventy years old when he hoisted the glass-football championship trophy the night of January 4, 2000, in New Orleans's Superdome, already had surpassed the likes of Woody Hayes and Bo Schembechler in Division 1-A victories. His footprints in the landscape of college football history would only sink deeper in subsequent seasons as he leapfrogged Amos Alonzo Stagg, Glenn "Pop" Warner, Paul "Bear" Bryant, and finally Joe Paterno to ascend to number one all-time among major-college coaches.

One year later a Florida State team would suit up for a climactic national championship game for the third consecutive year and the fifth time in eight seasons. The Seminoles would fall victim to the Oklahoma Sooners, 13–2, in a defensive slugfest in the Orange Bowl as different from the Virginia Tech shoot-out as soccer is from basketball.

But that 2000 season became the fourteenth in succession in which FSU achieved at least ten victories and finished number five or higher in the post-bowls Associated Press poll of sportswriters and sportscasters. Not only was the feat unprecedented, it's safe to say it will never be equaled. And that remarkable success starts with Bowden, who departed West Virginia for Florida State in 1976 thinking of the challenge in Tallahassee as a stepping-stone to a higher-profile coaching job.

You couldn't get much lower profile than FSU at the time. The teams coached by Larry Jones in 1973 and Darrell Mudra in 1974 and 1975 had combined for four victories in those three seasons. By painstaking count, twelve of Bowden's teams have since celebrated at least that many victories in the month of October alone.

Bowden often joked that when he coached at West Virginia in the early 1970s, fans' bumper stickers implored the Mountaineers, "Beat Pitt!" or "Beat Penn State!" Upon arrival at FSU, he punch-lined, he found bumper stickers begging that the Seminoles "Beat Anybody!"

But no coach excels without talented players, and no one has ever surpassed Bowden as a close-the-deal recruiter. Players who have paraded through the trophy-and-plaque-bejeweled atrium at Doak Campbell Stadium represent a *Who's Who* honor roll. Heisman Trophy winners Charlie Ward and Chris Weinke quarterbacked Bowden's two national title teams. Deion Sanders may be the greatest cornerback not only in collegiate lore but also in pro history. Sebastian Janikowski, a two-time winner of the Lou Groza award, ranks with the greatest college placekickers, and 1992 Butkus Award winner Marvin Jones is certainly on a par with the fiercest linebackers.

In a dozen National Football League drafts between 1989 and 2000, NFL commissioner Paul Tagliabue read the names of twenty Seminoles as first-round selections. In the 1997 draft alone, defensive end Peter Boulware, offensive tackle Walter Jones, running back Warrick Dunn, and defensive end Reinard Wilson became surefire millionaires before the fifteenth selection.

But none of them ever gave a more breathtaking performance for sixty minutes than Warrick did in his Sugar Bowl farewell performance after that turbulent year in his young life.

Warrick had served as a lightning rod for controversy during the 12–0 campaign, which was speckled with imperfections and one narrow escape after another. (Truth be told, Bowden's 1993 national championship team had been a far more dominating bunch in spite of a 31–24 loss at Notre Dame.)

Warrick served a two-game suspension and weathered three months of subsequent ridicule for his role in a Dillard's department store scam that also involved soon-banished teammate Laveranues Coles and a nineteen-year-old sales clerk who sold them $400 worth of designer clothing at the bargain rate of $21 and change. Though charges subsequently and appropriately were reduced to misdemeanor, a few indignant members of the national media believed Warrick should not have been allowed to play another down for FSU. They presumably would also urge that jaywalkers be sentenced to five years without parole.

Father-figure Bowden's well-documented proclivity for giving misbehaving players a second chance factored into the criticism. But to those who suggested that a two-game suspension and Warrick's financial restitution to the department store seemed lenient, Bowden firmly countered that it was only part of the punishment. "How about knocking him out of the Heisman Trophy race?" Bowden asked. "How about knocking him out of the Biletnikoff [awarded to the nation's premier wide receiver]? That was a gimme."

Bowden wasn't lying. In helmet and shoulder pads, Warrick transformed from lightning rod to lightning bolt. Never was that more evident than during that new-millennium night in New Orleans. The vision of Virginia Tech quarterback Michael Vick wreaking similar havoc on FSU's defense served only to add wattage to Warrick's electrifying exploits.

Warrick, contrite over the Dillard's episode that provided the only notable smudge on his FSU record, had expressed the desire

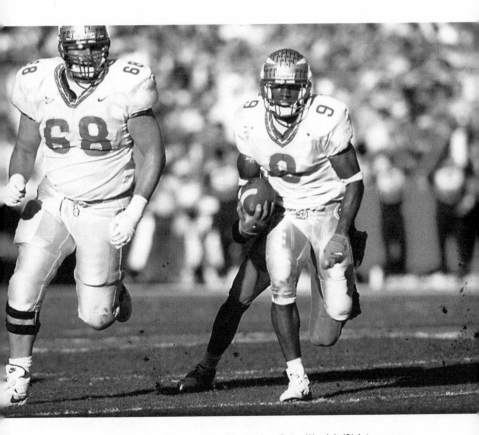

*Guard Jason Whitaker (68) convoys wide receiver Peter Warrick (9) into an open field during FSU's perfect 1999 championship season.*

in days before the Sugar Bowl showdown to do something to make fans "remember me for what I did on the field, not how I messed up off the field." Did he ever.

Too much play-by-play detail in a tome of this nature tends to make the eyes glaze over. So I'll offer that disclaimer up front and apply some restraint. But if any game in FSU history warrants replaying for posterity, the one that capped a perfect 12–0 season does. How often, after all, has any game showcasing two players with the extraordinary talents Warrick and Vick possess actually surpassed the grandiose expectations on such a huge stage and under such bright lights?

In the midst of the pregame hype, Bowden had observed, "When I first watched Vick play, I thought, 'Gee whiz, don't you wish you had a quarterback like that!' I got to thinking, 'Well, Peter Warrick is the same dadgummed [kind of threat].'"

Vick, a redshirt freshman in that Sugar Bowl, put on national display the dazzling blend of passing and running skills that would within five years make him the NFL's most exciting performer. Then, as later, his retreat into the pocket to pass prompted unspoken prayers by defensive coordinators that he "please throw the ball." Defenses tend to collapse when he takes flight to avoid a rush.

So do knees, by the way. Both linebacker Tommy Polley and defensive end Roland Seymour suffered severe knee injuries not while being blocked, but from quick twists or turns on unyielding Superdome turf trying to mirror Vick's dead-run zigs and zags.

The flow of the game bore as many sharp turns as Vick's jaunts. Typifying an early Virginia Tech haymaker that failed to land, Frank Beamer's Hokies snapped the ball on twenty of the first twenty-three offensive plays but failed to capitalize. On Beamer's fourth-down-and-one gamble from FSU's 3 yard line on Tech's opening drive, Seminole safety Derrick Gibson slashed through to slam Vick and shake loose a fumble that defensive tackle Corey Simon wrestled away from Hokies tailback Andre Kendrick in the end zone.

Weinke and Warrick then hooked up on the first of what would become bookend touchdown passes igniting and concluding 75 points of fireworks with 5 touchdown starbursts on plays of 43 yards or more. The shifty Warrick worked loose to snare a deep pass and sprint to a 64-yard score. The Seminoles then drew off to a 28–7 advantage with 3 more touchdowns within the next 6:22 of action.

Polley, as he had in FSU's 30–23 escape in the regular-season finale at Florida, blocked a punt, and reserve tailback Jeff Chaney corralled it on a bounce and dashed 6 yards into the end zone. Wide receiver Ron Dugans turned a third-down Weinke pass of 8 yards into a 63-yard score when a defensive back gambled for an interception and lost. Moments later, after Virginia Tech failed to advance, Warrick snatched a punt by Jimmy Kibble and returned it 59 yards to send signals of a blowout.

Check signals. Remember, Vick's on the other team. His 49-yard touchdown pass to wide receiver Andre Davis and a 3-yard stroll to climax a scoring drive just before intermission had Virginia Tech within 28–14 striking distance.

The third quarter belonged to Vick and Virginia Tech. Ike Charlton dizzied Seminoles who tried to cover punts with returns of 23 and 46 yards. Shayne Graham kicked a 23-yard field goal. Anthony Midget intercepted a Weinke bomb. And

Kendrick scored from 29 yards out with a slickly executed option pitch from Vick and later on a 6-yard run after Vick had sucked the air right out of the Superdome with scrambles covering 15 and 22 yards. (Vick finished the night with 225 yards passing and 97 running.)

Two-point passes failed after the Kendrick touchdowns that first carved FSU's advantage to 28–23 and then produced Tech's 29–28 advantage. Still, the Seminoles had been rocked so far back on their heels that Bowden was forced to revert to the "riverboat gambler" mode that marked his early coaching years, when he did not have the talent to play it straight.

On the next possession, FSU stalled at its own 46 yard line and confronted fourth down needing a yard to retain possession. The punting team remained on the sideline. "They had momentum," Bowden explained afterwards, "and if we had to punt to them one more time, I don't know if we would ever have gotten momentum back . . . Our defense couldn't stop 'em."

Enter Marcus Outzen. The red-haired reserve called "Rooster" had been pressed into starting duty late the previous season when Weinke suffered a spinal injury that nearly ended his career. Outzen proved to be functional in a 24–7 victory at Wake Forest and a 23–12 upset of Florida in which Warrick both threw and caught touchdown passes. But Outzen's misplays in only his third career start doomed the Seminoles to a 23–16 national-championship loss to Tennessee in the Fiesta Bowl.

Here he was a year later, inserted for Weinke on a play that could determine victory or defeat because he had quicker feet and a keener sense of where to dive on a quarterback sneak. Only he didn't sneak. Offensive coordinator Mark Richt, who in 2001 would become head coach at the University of Georgia, persuaded Bowden instead to rubber-stamp a pitchout. Tailback Travis Minor got to the outside, twice spun 360 degrees, and netted 16 critical yards before a late-hit penalty tacked on 15 more.

Minor's run highlighted the eleven-play, 85-yard drive that culminated in Weinke's 14-yard scoring pass to Dugans and triggered FSU's 18-point fourth-quarter response to Virginia Tech's 15-point third quarter. Another fumble by the overworked Vick and a fake punt that failed kept the Hokies from answering back. To review: The Seminoles scored on a blocked punt and a punt return and foiled a fake punt against a coach, Frank Beamer, whose special teams always have been extra special.

The backfiring fake punt gave FSU possession at Virginia Tech's 43 yard line with a 39–29 lead and set the stage for Warrick's final dagger. "Coach told me the play was going to be a 'takeoff,'" Warrick said. "I knew the ball was coming to me. It was a one-man route."

That's when he entered the huddle and, for all practical purposes, called his shot. Bowden affirmed the sideline exchange. Guard Jason Whitaker verified Warrick's words in the huddle. The ensuing play is one of those you want to witness repeatedly on instant replay to see if your eyes have betrayed you.

Hokies cornerback Ronyell Whitaker sprinted step for step with Warrick toward the goal line. Weinke's heave led them perfectly. Whitaker raked his right arm across the top of both of Warrick's arms as Warrick turned his head and reached out. Warrick's left hand tipped the ball, and as he was falling onto his left side away from the defender, he freed his arms to momentarily juggle and then secure the ball to his body. The declined pass-

# A-Plus for Move to ACC

Arrogance fueled Southeastern Conference bigwigs' belief during the summer of 1990 that, given a choice between membership in the SEC or the Atlantic Coast Conference, Florida State would perform cartwheels of glee into the SEC. But FSU president Bernie Sliger and athletic director Bob Goin, weighing significant financial and academic ramifications, opted for FSU to become the giant pawn in Commissioner Gene Corrigan's quest to upgrade ACC football.

The courtship that preceded the marriage had its amusing aspects. Neither the SEC nor the ACC wanted to extend an invitation without being assured the answer would be affirmative. FSU didn't want to reveal a preference before a proposal was assured.

Goin's analogy before Corrigan twisted a few wrists to get the six votes required for ACC expansion still rings true and evokes a chuckle. "I've looked across the dance floor a lot of times, when I was a young boy in high school and wanted to ask a girl to dance," Goin said that summer. "But I was afraid if I walked all the way across that floor and asked, I might get told, 'Get lost.' What you did was have a friend go over and ask her, 'Would you dance with him if he asked you?'"

Laughing, Goin concluded, "That's the way conferences work."

interference penalty would have produced 15 yards. Warrick's determination produced 43 yards and the final margin.

For the fourth time in the Seminoles' final five games, Weinke had rallied FSU from a deficit in the second half. Key, of course, was his maturity. He was twenty-seven years old. He did

Subsequent accusations that FSU simply feared the level of football competition in the SEC were disingenuous. The Seminoles played Florida annually anyway and had a new home-and-home contract to play Auburn every season through 1999. In the SEC's realignment, FSU would have met Auburn only twice every eight years but would have played Kentucky and Vanderbilt every year along with Florida, Georgia, and Tennessee.

During the 1989 season, the Seminoles had played and defeated Auburn, Florida, and Louisiana State, as well as South Carolina, which filled the void as the SEC's twelfth member after FSU committed to the ACC. Clemson, from the ACC, dealt FSU a loss.

In 1990, still a football independent but now engaged to the ACC, FSU beat LSU, Florida, and South Carolina and lost to Auburn, which then hastily bailed out of the final nine years of the deal with FSU. It was coincidental that ACC teams posted victories in all four games against SEC teams during the 1990 regular season and that the ACC's Georgia Tech capped a 10-0-1 regular season with a 40-23 rout of Georgia and claimed a share of the national championship with a 45-21 Citrus Bowl romp past Nebraska.

SEC football superiority was acknowledged then and continued until the ACC added Miami, Virginia Tech, and Boston College in recent seasons. But the difference never was as great as SEC proponents believed.

not take his first class at FSU until after a six-year professional baseball career that peaked at Class AAA, and then only briefly.

Chris Fowler and the ESPN Game Day crew later interviewed Most Valuable Player Warrick on a stage set up in the corner of the end zone. He openly addressed the subject of the off-field misadventure that stained his season and effectively aborted any shot at a Heisman Trophy. "I learned I'm like a fish in a fishbowl," he said. "I know that every time I go out, I've got to do what's right because I've got a lot of kids looking up to me. I don't want that bad image on me."

Warrick could have entered the NFL draft after his 1998 junior season. The consensus was that he would have been taken early in the first round and likely would have received a signing bonus upwards of $5 million. But he put the NFL on hold to complete his Florida State career. Otherwise there would have been no furor over a clothing purchase in which a little over $21 changed hands instead of $400.

"I came back [for a senior season] because I love Coach Bowden and I love everybody on the team with us," Warrick told the ESPN crew. "When I got in that trouble, Coach Bowden stepped it up for me. I won this game for him."

On a reflective note, to me Warrick always came across as a kid with a great personality, as someone playful and mischievous. However, in no way can you write off the Dillard's episode as mischief. It was a monumental lapse in judgment. But it did not typify his character. What Warrick discovered in the aftermath is that the larger the pedestal you climb, the more eager critics are to take a jackhammer to it. I always thought he handled himself well in the harsh spotlight that resulted.

Bowden's second national championship did not end the remarkable streak that kept the Seminoles in the midst of the title fight for fourteen consecutive seasons. Weinke returned in 2000 to win the Heisman Trophy and propel those once-beaten Seminoles into the Orange Bowl against the Oklahoma Sooners with

*Peter Warrick (left) celebrates FSU's 46–29 national championship victory over Virginia Tech with coach Bobby Bowden.*

at least a share of the championship within reach.

The Sooners' 13–2 victory in a game that showcased defensive grit as impressive as the offensive wizardry in the previous year's Sugar Bowl foretold a change in fortunes. The departure of Richt for Georgia, Weinke for the NFL, and fifteen other starters prompted an ensuing return to the "normalcy" in which a three- or four-loss season was dismissed as failure by fans so spoiled by success for so long.

Think about it. During those fourteen consecutive seasons that culminated in postbowls rankings in the top five, next-best Miami finished fifth or better seven times; Nebraska and Florida five times; and Colorado, Michigan, and Notre Dame four times. From 1987 forward, all of the above except FSU also endured a stretch of four or more consecutive seasons in which they failed to finish in the top ten.

For some time the NCAA designated "dynasties" in its record book. Between 1981 and 2000, four were cited: Miami from 1983 through 1992, a span that included four championships; Florida from 1990 through 1999 under Steve Spurrier; Nebraska from 1988 to 1997; and FSU's.

Florida State's schedule includes Miami and Florida every single year with a trip to either Miami or Gainesville. That practically ensures a loss every season. It's not coincidental that FSU's two national-championship campaigns featured victories over Spurrier's Gators in Gainesville. (Spurrier never did beat Bowden in Tallahassee.)

Also, four of the fourteen seasons of FSU dominance concluded with bowl matchups against Tom Osborne's Nebraska Cornhuskers. The Seminoles won all four. The 18–16 Orange Bowl showdown that determined the 1993 national champion was perceived by many as a flawed performance by once-beaten FSU, though Nebraska was undefeated and ranked number one to FSU's number two in the Bowl Coalition standings. History softened that perception. Nebraska didn't lose again until two and a half years and two national championships later.

Mickey Andrews, the architect of FSU's defenses throughout the era of excellence, played at Alabama for Coach Bryant amidst early-1960s supremacy that resulted in three national championships in a five-year span. He has a solid platform from which to compare two coaching legends. "Football has changed a lot, the way people do things scheme-wise," he said late in the 2000 season. "But the way you win hasn't changed. Coach Bryant knew what it took to win at that time. Coach Bowden knows what it takes to win now."

Bowden, a man unburdened by ego, would not dare to enter a debate over who is the best coach ever. But the record books show that no one in major college football has ever won more.

# Hangin' with Legends

Florida State University will forever owe a debt of gratitude to the anonymous pranksters at West Virginia who demonstrated their displeasure over the Mountaineers' 1974 struggles by hanging the football coach in effigy. West Virginia coach Bobby Bowden posted a 42–26 record in the six years after he succeeded Jim Carlen in Morgantown. But that 1974 season became a career pothole that was treated as a sinkhole by critics. West Virginia suffered through a 4–7 campaign that season and alerted Bowden to the precarious career path he had chosen.

Years later he was fuzzy on what specifically prompted critics to dangle a dummy bearing his name from a tree limb about a block from the stadium. But he did recall that year as "one of the lowest periods of my life."

The "hanging" wasn't an isolated act of disgruntlement. "There were editorials in the student newspaper saying I ought to go," he recalled. "I saw sheets hanging out of dorm windows with 'Bye-bye, Bobby' written on them. Believe me, you get mentally tough when that happens."

In today's age of multiyear contracts and automatic rollover clauses, a coach could shrug off a subpar season as a blip on the screen, an aberration that could be rectified by a winning record the next fall. Bowden, however, had no such security. West Virginia statutes at the time limited contracts to one year. That applied to the university president as well as the football coach.

Bowden's Mountaineers rebounded for a nine-victory season in 1975, capping it with a 13–10 victory over North Carolina State in the Peach Bowl. All was forgiven in Morgantown. But Bowden hadn't forgotten.

Bowden traveled to Tampa a week after the bowl to coach in the short-lived All-America all-star game. John Bridgers, Florida State's athletic director at the time, had telephoned Bowden during the season to assess whether he might be interested in a change of scenery. Bridgers contacted him again in Tampa and persuaded Bowden and his wife, Ann, to visit Tallahassee on the way back to West Virginia. They liked what they saw. West Virginia's loss became FSU's gain.

Several years later, after Bowden had made FSU matter nationally with back-to-back seasons culminating in Orange

Bowl battles with Barry Switzer's Oklahoma Sooners, he joked about the comfort of security. "They may hang me here, too," he quipped, "but it will cost them a whole lot more to cut me down."

For what Bowden has achieved in thirty seasons at FSU, it's far more likely that his image would be carved into the face of a mountain alongside those of Knute Rockne, Paul "Bear" Bryant, and Joe Paterno than that he'd be strung up in effigy again.

In some ways the 1993 and 1999 national championships Florida State has celebrated, while undeniably necessary to Bowden's legacy, are incidental to the unmatched achievement of keeping the Seminoles in the heat of a national championship fight for fourteen consecutive seasons.

Alumni and boosters become so accustomed to great success that they forget what failure looks like. That's human nature. Any fan who attended every home game in the 1990s saw the Seminoles lose once. Only in that context can an 8–4 season be perceived as a disappointment.

Resistance to the inevitable tug of parity over an extended period would be unfathomable, except that Bowden's teams from 1987 through 2000 successfully resisted. FSU athletic director Dave Hart said to me for a 1999 article, "I'm not sure any of us truly appreciate what a phenomenal accomplishment we're living [through] here."

That's partly attributable to Bowden's own reaction. He has never become puffed up with power or preened with chest-thumping pride. No one succeeds as Bowden has without a healthy self-esteem. But if you put off your next meal until you detect ego in Bowden, you'll starve.

He always has freely exercised a self-deprecating wit, and

over the last ten to fifteen seasons, he has passed himself off as more of a CEO than a hands-on coach. Contrasted to how involved he was back in the 1960s and 1970s, that probably seems an accurate depiction to him. But don't be deceived. He meets with coaches and players. He studies film. He watches practice from a tower, yes, but he's frequently scribbling notes to himself that dictate his postpractice message. Even at seventy-six, he's no figurehead.

He undoubtedly delegates now more than he did in the 1980s. And when FSU graduated to perennial power in the late 1980s, Bowden no longer had to lean toward shock-value play-calling so regularly. At one point early in his career, the Seminoles ran the reverse with a wide receiver so routinely that Bowden no longer thought of it as a trick play. But the superior force rarely has to trade on trickery, and Bowden built FSU into a superior program.

As former athletic director Bob Goin once said, Bobby Bowden *is* Florida State football. And the benefit extends beyond what happens on that 100-yard-long rectangle of grass or phony turf. The man is as impressive as the record. He's as common as the record is uncommon. (Bowden wrapped up a congratulatory telephone call from President Bill Clinton with "See ya', Buddy.")

I've always said that I've never met anyone more comfortable in his own skin. That still holds true today. Getting a paycheck for covering Bowden's FSU teams from 1981 through 2000 was, in some respects, like stealing money. On the Sunday morning after a home game, you'd walk into the "Breakfast with Bobby" sessions at a Tallahassee hotel and let him fill your notebook while he both enlightened and entertained you.

*Bobby Bowden (at podium) shares a laugh with President Bill Clinton and FSU president Sandy D'Alemberte (right) at a White House celebration of a national title.*

I've watched his teams win games they shouldn't have. I've watched his teams lose games they shouldn't have. I've marveled at his flair for the unexpected. I've second-guessed play calls and clock management at the end of a game. The only way not to make mistakes is not to make decisions. I won't suggest he's the greatest coach who ever lived. (Neither will he.) But he walks with the legends of the game. Don't ever forget the depths to which Florida State football had plummeted before he arrived.

The three seasons prior to Bowden's rule produced 0–11, 1–10, and 3–8 records. The reversal of fortunes was not immediate. Bowden's first FSU team started 0–3, including a 47–0 thrashing at Miami. A 33–26 home-field loss to Florida triggered another three-game losing streak that left the Seminoles 2–6 on the season and 2–16–1 in the lopsided series with the Gators.

But three consecutive victories, none by more than 7 points, rallied the 1976 Seminoles to a 5–6 record. No Bowden team since has finished with a losing record. Still, even after his 1977 Seminoles capped a 10–2 season with a 40–17 Tangerine Bowl victory over Texas Tech, few would have expected that Florida State would attain a stature to rival that of Notre Dame, Southern Cal, Ohio State, Nebraska, and Alabama at their glorious best.

## What You See Is What You Get

I've certainly encountered Bowden detractors over the years. But the primary criticism—an erroneous one—has been that nobody can be as unfailingly pleasant, positive, and accessible as Bowden appears. These rare critics should get to know him better.

Appearances do not deceive. Bowden is who he is: a man who climbed the coaching ladder from the bottom rung; a hero-worshipper as a youth who still has a hard time coming to grips with the idea that he has become a hero to many; a clever football tactician willing to take a chance; a motivational speaker and quick-witted raconteur who is always willing to poke fun at himself; a religious man as comfortable in a pulpit as he is in a

*Ann Bowden (right) is undeniably the matriarch of the First Family of coaching. She helped raise two sons who, like their father, each coached college teams to perfect seasons.*

recruit's living room; and, above all, a family man devoted to his wife and six children.

To get a greater sense of the man, you'd have to listen to the anecdotes, to the comments and snatches of conversation culled from two decades, and to the words of his admirers. For example, Bowden himself traces his own outgoing nature to his father. "My daddy never met a stranger. He really liked people, and he was uninhibited. If he wanted to sing, he'd just break out and start singing. He didn't care what people might think. He just had a good time. He enjoyed life."

Bowden, who was raised in Birmingham, Alabama, developed a boyhood fascination with the football legends of the 1940s when he was bedridden with what was diagnosed as rheumatic fever. "I used to keep scrapbooks as a boy. I bet I've got twenty to thirty [newspaper] pictures of Doc Blanchard and Glenn Davis, Mr. Inside and Mr. Outside for the great Army teams."

A fascination with military history also evolved from news from World War II battlefronts, when the stricken Bowden's primary connection to the outside world was a radio. "All my life I've found studying generals fascinating. I guess there are two extremes. There's the one who stays static all the time. Won't try anything. Sits there and defends and digs in and builds his fortifications like he's supposed to . . . Then there's the guy who will take chances and is daring. He'll slip around to your flank. He'll attack you in broad daylight when you think he wouldn't dare. They're the ones who are very aggressive. They're gamblers, your Pattons and Rommels and Robert E. Lees."

Bowden's imaginative approach to football draws from military leaders' approach to combat. But it also derives from his youth. "Playing football when I was a kid, it seems I was always smaller playing with older guys. Then, when I went to Howard College, we always were playing schools much bigger than us. We were always underdogs."

Bowden will tell you he developed audacity to offset his own lack of size or an opponent's superior forces. He grinned delightedly in this elaboration. "To explain the word *audacity*, I've always reminded folks of the old Red Skelton television shows.

Somebody would come up with a water pistol, fixin' to shoot him, and Ol' Red would do this double take and say, 'YOU WOULDN'T DARE!' Like in football, you wouldn't DARE run a reverse on third down near your own goal line." Bowden laughed. "Oh yes, we will! Oh yes, we will!"

Because Notre Dame games were broadcast nationally, he became as familiar with the Irish as he was with Alabama and Auburn. "My first Notre Dame hero was [1943 Heisman Trophy–winning quarterback] Angelo Bertelli. I got to meet him in 1993 when Charlie Ward became a Heisman winner, and I was invited to the banquet. Seeing [Bertelli] and Leon Hart, all the old Notre Damers, was a thrill for me."

Bowden paid a price back in college for his reluctance to cut his losses and retreat when confronted by formidable odds. For a guy who loved to gamble on the football field, he admits he took a beating from friends and teammates at the card table. "I'd be the poorest gambler at the table. I learned then not to play poker. I could never win. And the reason is I would never fold. I couldn't stand to leave my money out on that table."

After his 1953 graduation from Howard College, Bowden's coaching travelogue began at his alma mater, took him to South Georgia Junior College from 1956 to 1958, returned him to Howard (now Samford) as head coach from 1959 through 1962, landed him at Florida State as an assistant to Bill Peterson from 1963 through 1965, and then took him to West Virginia as Jim Carlen's offensive coordinator from 1966 until he became head coach in 1970. Early in that career journey, Bowden worried that he wasn't as upwardly mobile as he'd like to be. Wife Ann suggested that he might seem more seasoned and mature to potential employers if he went by the proper name Robert. But Bowden figured if the more familiar reference was good enough for famed Georgia Tech coach Bobby Dodd, it was good enough for him. He's not one for pretense or formality. Bobby's the right fit.

Bowden will tell you he did not picture Florida State as a lifetime job. He thought it would be another stepping-stone toward the position he'd dreamed about as a boy—head coach at Alabama. Bear Bryant was, and remains, a heroic figure to him. Bridgers invited Bryant to a golf outing in Tallahassee after the 1977 season. Bowden, trying unsuccessfully to minimize what it meant to him, once told me, "We played golf. We talked football. And [Bryant] said, 'I'm keeping my eye on you.' He didn't say why. Just 'I'm keeping my eye on you.'"

Indeed Bowden found himself in the middle of a media furor in Birmingham in December 1986 after his Seminoles had defeated Indiana in the since-defunct All-America Bowl. Ray Perkins, successor to Bryant after the 1982 season, resigned at Alabama to coach the NFL's Tampa Bay Buccaneers. Unofficial representatives of the university sounded out Bowden about whether he'd be interested in the vacancy. Essentially, Bowden's reply was that he'd be interested if somebody made an official and firm offer but that he didn't plan to pursue the job. Driving from Birmingham back to Tallahassee the day after the bowl, he realized what a circus the speculation was creating and squelched it with word that he'd be staying at Florida State. Subsequently, he admitted that by that point, he thought his Seminoles were better positioned to chase the national championship than storied Alabama. The 1986 season was the last until 2001 in which FSU did not appear in the national title picture.

Recruiting is the first step toward the kind of success Bowden has enjoyed ever since. Even today no coach can match the combined aura and comfort with which Bowden enters a prospect's living room to court him and his parents. Former assistant Brad Scott once explained Bowden's effectiveness this way: "Coach Bowden doesn't go into a player's home with a canned sales pitch. He's just Bobby Bowden. He's sincere. He's genuine. And parents understand that that's the same Bobby Bowden they've seen on TV. He relaxes them."

Bowden also identifies with parents. "I don't try to paint a phony picture. I let the parents know I had six children who graduated from college and that I know how important it is to them that their kids get degrees."

In Bowden's mind, successful recruitment of a teenager brings a responsibility to perform as surrogate parent. Former fullback William Floyd, who never knew his real father, said late in an FSU career that propelled him into the pros, "I go straight to the man when I have some problem . . . I look on Coach Bowden as a father figure." That was true as well of Warrick Dunn, who, after the shooting death of his police-officer mother, took on the daunting role of head of household for his brothers and sisters. He often sought Bowden's counsel.

Teenagers do get into trouble. It's sometimes difficult to balance whether Bowden has more players who tilt toward problems than those in other programs or whether there's simply a brighter and sometimes harsher spotlight shined on the Miamis and Nebraskas and Ohio States because they've sat on college football's throne. But the perception that Bowden is permissive is fueled by his tendency to give a youth a second chance. Critics,

# Losing FSU Football: Ancient History

The last time Florida State endured a losing football season was in 1976, and it was the only time under Coach Bobby Bowden. Here's just a small sample of what else was happening way back when.

- Jimmy Carter, a peanut farmer and former governor of the state of Georgia, had just been elected president of the United States, ending the two-year stewardship of Gerald Ford brought on by Richard Nixon's Watergate.

- Boxer Sugar Ray Leonard won the gold medal in the light-welterweight class in the Olympic Games in Montreal, but the Olympian who stole American hearts was an eighty-three-pound Romanian gymnast named Nadia Comeneci.

- Sylvester Stallone wrote the script and starred in the blockbuster film Rocky, about a small-time Philadelphia boxer who belted his way to glory . . . and then did it again and again and again and again through who knows how many sequels.

- Pete Rose, Joe Morgan, Tony Perez, and the rest of Sparky Anderson's Cincinnati Reds swept the New York Mets in four games to win the World Series; Morgan and New York Yankees catcher Thurman Munson were voted Most Valuable Players for the National and American League.

- Heisman Trophy winner Tony Dorsett rushed for 2,130 yards and 23 touchdowns as the University of Pittsburgh, coached by Johnny Majors, romped to a 12–0 record and national championship secured by a 27–3 Sugar Bowl rout of Georgia.

- Bob Knight's Indiana Hoosiers, led by Kent Benson and Quinn Buckner, completed a perfect season with an 86–68 NCAA championship–game romp past Big Ten rival Michigan.

That all seems so long ago. And Bowden keeps on fielding winning teams.

however, don't balance that with recognition that FSU dismissed two of the top pass catchers in the NFL—Oakland's Randy Moss and the New York Jets' Laveranues Coles—from the program. Moss, who arrived under a cloud, never played a down. Bowden's slant: "I've always said I'd give them a second chance, but you won't hear of me giving them a third. I do believe in forgiveness, but I've got other kids who have to know there's a program [with rules] here."

Any study of Bowden without an appreciation for his ever-present sense of humor would do him as much an injustice as a failure to recognize his innate decency and sense of fair play. You could write a book on his humorous stories and inevitable one-liners. I remember him talking after the 1992 season about whether all-world linebacker Marvin Jones, a junior who had just won both the Butkus and Lombardi awards, would be back for his senior season. He expected Jones to depart but added, "I say that, hoping lightning will strike and that Marvin will say, 'I LOVE school! I LOVE room, board, tuition, and books. I HATE income taxes.'"

Tulane coach Wally English went to court against the NCAA and received a temporary judgment that allowed his son, Jon—a quarterback who by 1983 had been enrolled at Michigan State, Iowa State, and two junior colleges—to play against the Seminoles. Tulane notched a 34–28 victory (later forfeited). Bowden's conclusion: "We've got to do a better job defending the injunction."

Another of my favorites has to do with Louisiana State's refusal in 1982 to move a traditional nighttime kickoff to afternoon so that CBS could televise the game. That move cost FSU's program a financial windfall. Bowden was upset. "I don't see how we can cry about our economic problems [in college athletics] and turn down television paydays. I also don't see how you can build a national championship program and not be on TV." He asked reporters how much FSU would have received from CBS. He was told $550,000. He did one of his own Red Skelton double takes and said, "I'm madder than I thought."

Family, naturally, also provides grist for Bowden's wit. Wife Ann simply smiles and rolls her eyes when Bowden tells booster club audiences she's a member of the MasterCard Hall of Fame. Steve Bowden, the only one of the Bowdens' four sons not to go into coaching, planned to be on Clemson's sideline with brother Tommy for the historic first father-son coaching collision in 1999. Bowden noted that and said, "Don't forget to remind me to strike him from the will."

Sons Terry and Tommy both have coached teams to perfect seasons: Terry in his first at Auburn in 1993 and Tommy in his last at Tulane in 1998 before Clemson courted and hired him. But no situation ever better reflected the short attention span of boosters who take a proprietary approach to programs than the unseemly circumstances of Terry's resignation at Auburn in 1998. He sported a 45–12–1 record before a tumultuous 1–5 start that year. But meddling boosters and a disloyal assistant provoked Terry Bowden to walk away before he was fired. Tommy Bowden's stay at Clemson, while successful, also has not been without a need to extinguish the odd brushfire of discontent. But even in his sons' periodic and inevitable coaching lows, Bobby Bowden has taken comfort in this: "When a coach's son goes into coaching, he knows the pitfalls . . . I've always told them there are two kinds of coaches: ones that have been fired and ones that haven't been fired *yet*. It's a cliché, but it's true."

The only shadow cast over Bowden's 75–10 record from 1987 through the 1993 regular season was the glaring absence of a national championship. Observers assumed that must have driven Bowden nuts. It didn't. It truly didn't. His focus always had been on winning the next game, and the next, and the next. He once explained: "I believe I would rather go 10–1, 10–1, 10–1 for five years and never win the championship than go 5–6, 5–6, national championship, 5–6, 5–6. I'd go crazy. I'd shoot myself those other four years. I'd be a dead man with a national championship."

The infectious laughter that accompanied his "dead man" punch line is the whimsical flip side of the reality that faces us all. Bowden becomes reflective when someone raises the subject of retirement from the coaching career that has rewarded him with a prominent place in football lore. He recalls his hero, Bear Bryant, who died only a month after he retired. Bowden's conclusion: "After you retire, there's only one big event left."

# "C. W." for Heisman

They have little more in common than the initials "C. W.," the national championships they brought to Florida State University, and the cherished trophy to which their names will be affixed for their lifetimes and beyond. One is African-American, the other Caucasian. One is from Thomasville, Georgia, the other from St. Paul, Minnesota. One practically shaped the athletic quarterback mold from which marvelous Michael Vick emerged at Virginia Tech years later; the other stood tall in the pocket as a classic drop-back passer. But possibly the most intriguing and revealing contrast between quarter-backs Charlie Ward and Chris Weinke involved timing and athletic versatility.

Weinke had played professional baseball for six years before he won the Heisman Trophy. Ward, within months of accepting college football's most coveted individual award, opted to apply his extraordinary talents to professional basketball.

Six summers in the Toronto Blue Jays' farm system did not produce the rapid rise and the rewards Weinke had anticipated when he chose baseball and a healthy signing bonus over a Florida State football scholarship. He did briefly reach Class AAA. But a growing realization that he'd likely not get to the majors prompted him to scrape rust off skills that in 1989 made him the number one high school quarterback in the land.

Ward didn't have to abandon one sport for another at FSU. With Bobby Bowden's blessing, he played two. While serving an apprenticeship that had become a pattern for Bowden's quarterbacks and before he became the catalyst for a fast-break football offense blueprinted to his skills, Ward executed fast breaks as point guard for Pat Kennedy's FSU basketball team. Without him, it's safe to say, the Seminoles would not have defeated perennial championship contender North Carolina twice during the regular season and reached the 1992 NCAA Sweet Sixteen before bowing to Bob Knight's Indiana Hoosiers.

Predictably, given their success, Ward and Weinke did share a couple of other attributes. Though not at all alike in personality, both demonstrated natural leadership traits. And neither was easily rattled by adversity, even when their initial outings as Florida State's starting quarterback raised red flags of doubt.

*Heisman Trophy winners Charlie Ward (left) and Chris Weinke flank Bobby Bowden, whose Florida State teams they quarterbacked to a pair of national championships.*

Fortunately, Bowden was no quicker to panic than Ward and Weinke. Had he overreacted to Ward's early struggles at the controls in 1992 or Weinke's in 1998, Florida State's 1993 and 1999 national championship trophies might be on display on campuses elsewhere.

Ward suffered 8 interceptions in his first two starts. As late as the seventh game of the 1992 season, Bowden briefly benched Ward at Georgia Tech to allow him to get his bearings in the midst of a shaky performance that helped saddle the Seminoles with a 21–7 deficit in the fourth quarter. But that's when FSU's fast break was born. Ward, typically unshaken, personally ran or passed for 206 of FSU's 207 yards in a no-huddle, 22-point blitz that salvaged a 29–24 victory.

"That game's when we said, 'Hey, that's Charlie's thing,'" Bowden said later. "That's when we decided to open up games in the shotgun and quit punting." Well, he didn't mean they'd *quit* punting. They just didn't have to punt very often.

During the week of the 27–14 Orange Bowl victory over Nebraska that capped Ward's 11–1 junior season, departing center Robbie Baker said, "This isn't Florida State's team any more. This is Charlie Ward's team. He's remarkable. He's going to lead us to a national championship." Baker's crystal ball was working.

A nightmarish 6 interceptions in Weinke's second collegiate start, at North Carolina State in 1998, doomed FSU to a 24–7 defeat and prompted questions about whether his lengthy sabbatical in baseball had eroded his football prowess. But Weinke passed for 17 touchdowns without a single interception in the next seven and a half games.

At that point, against Virginia, he suffered the neck injury that ended his 1998 season and arguably cost FSU the national title. But the injury and recovery gave storybook status to what he achieved first in the 1999 campaign and then in his Heisman-winning 2000 season.

Bowden already had witnessed in 1998 the maturity he anticipated in Weinke's refusal to choke on a momentary failure. So had teammates. They believed that Weinke would counter a crisis. Four times in the final five victories of FSU's perfect 1999 season, the Seminoles trailed at some point in the second half.

"Sometimes you have a leader on offense that the offense will follow," Bowden reflected. "Sometimes you'll have a leader on defense that the defense will follow. Weinke is a player *all* of them follow."

# Let Charlie Be Charlie

Mark Richt stood in a Dallas hotel in December 1991 and looked beyond the upcoming Cotton Bowl victory over Texas A&M that would return a bit of joy to a season launched by ten straight victories (none by fewer than 11 points) and then ruined by devastating 17–16 and 14–9 losses to Miami and Florida.

Richt, the quarterbacks coach at the time, knew the Seminoles would be replacing not only Heisman Trophy runner-up Casey Weldon (another "C. W.") but also erstwhile starter Brad Johnson. But his enthusiasm for the challenge ahead couldn't have been more genuine or infectious. On deck was a multitalented fourth-year junior who had patiently waited his turn.

Richt said he was eager to see what "number 17" could do at the controls. Asked if he had "a Darian Hagan with an arm," referencing Colorado's elusive quarterback, Richt countered, "A Jim Kelly with feet."

Richt, who was the backup University of Miami quarterback to future Buffalo Bills great Kelly in the early 1980s, recognized that because of Charlie Ward's quickness and mobility on a basketball court, some saw him as a running threat first and a passing threat second. Richt knew better. Indeed, of greater import than either his feet or his arm may have been Ward's instincts and poise.

Bowden's confidence in Ward before he ever started a football game grew from his decision to allow Ward to play basketball while he was serving a football apprenticeship first behind Peter Tom Willis and then Johnson and Weldon.

"What if Charlie hadn't played basketball?" Bowden asked rhetorically before the 1992 season. "Then I'm sitting here thinking, 'Ooooh, I wonder if he can handle pressure? Ooooh, I wonder what he's going to do on third down and nine? Ooooh, I wonder how he's going to play in the last minute [with a game on the line]?'

"I already have my answers—from basketball. I've seen his leadership. I've seen how he handles himself in front of big crowds. I've seen his ability to make things happen."

No less an authority, North Carolina coaching legend Dean Smith concurred. FSU made its Atlantic Coast Conference basketball debut in Chapel Hill, North Carolina, in December 1991. Though Seminoles star Doug Edwards was suspended for his role in a brawl in the previous game, Ward masterminded an 86–74 upset of the Tar Heels, who were ranked number five. Smith raved afterwards about Ward, who complemented 18 points with 5 rebounds, 4 assists, and 2 steals.

Two months later in Tallahassee, the Seminoles romped in the rematch, a 110–96 rout in which Ward contributed 9 assists and 6 steals. In his congratulatory remarks, Smith said, almost as an afterthought but with feeling, "And you *know* what I think of Charlie Ward."

Statistics did not reflect Ward's floor generalship. But it's worth noting that in FSU's initial appearance in the sacrosanct ACC postseason tournament, he engineered a 93–80 victory over North Carolina State with 13 points, 8 assists, 6 steals, and 7 rebounds.

But Ward was even more magical with a football in his hands. Even in his second consecutive 4-interception start in 1992, his confidence was unwavering. FSU trailed Clemson, 20–17, when it took possession at its own 23 yard line with 5:26 left. Ward proceeded to complete all five of his passes in a win-

*Charlie Ward was equally dangerous as a passer and runner in his two sensational seasons at FSU.*

ning eight-play drive culminating in his 9-yard scoring strike to Kevin Knox.

Five games later, at Georgia Tech, Ward's two third-quarter interceptions helped stake the Yellow Jackets to a 21–7 advantage and prompted a cameo series for freshman backup Danny Kanell. Ward returned unburdened by his mistakes. Bowden dictated that the Seminoles operate from their "one-minute" offense for the rest of the game. Voilá! A 29–24 victory. A new offense. Charlie Ward's trademark. And the genesis of the national championship season to follow.

Even in the midst of FSU's lone loss in 1993, a 31–24 setback at Notre Dame that momentarily stalled the charge, Ward was pitching into the end zone on the final play and trying to atone for a wind-buffeted and subpar passing performance. But the perspective that enabled him to cope with pressure also revealed itself when he was confronted by failure. Smiling wryly at somber questions that gave greater import to the setback than he thought warranted, Ward said, "This is a game. This isn't life and death. Nobody died out there."

Bowden observed after one of Ward's rescue efforts, "Does his temperament help the team? It's got to. It helps the *coaches*. Charlie isn't going to worry about anything. When he experiences devastation, it doesn't faze him one little bit."

That held true right up through the last-minute, penalty-abetted drive to Scott Bentley's winning field goal in the 18–16 Orange Bowl victory over Nebraska that produced, finally, Bowden's overdue national championship. Along the way, Ward flipped a pass to freshman Warrick Dunn for a 23-yard gain that became 38 when a 15-yard personal-foul penalty for a late hit was assessed. As receiver Matt Frier often had observed at fitting moments, "Charlie's as cool as Kool-Aid." So it was that night when Nebraska's defense threw him off his game.

For the record, the Heisman Trophy voting was no contest. Ward's name showed up number one on 740 of 813 ballots (which made you wonder what planet seventy-three of the voters inhabited the previous three months). That's 91 percent. The previous record was Desmond Howard's 85-percent dominance of 1991 voting. But rare athletic ability was only part of what made the future New York Knicks point guard so special.

To describe someone as even a better person than he is an athlete has become a cliché. But it was a toss-up whether Ward, raised in the Baptist faith by his parents and schooled in modesty, was more impressive in or out of uniform. Kennedy observed, "Charlie has developed this mystique. People wonder, 'Is he really that good of a person?' But there's no crack in the armor."

A locker room can get rowdy, the banter crude. But when Ward was nearby, a sports publicist once told me, the players around him automatically edited their language and toned down the ribaldry so as not to offend him. That's respect.

Ward's solid-citizen reputation moved in lockstep with his growing fame. After the 1992 football season and during the 1992–93 basketball season, Kennedy's Seminoles had travel connections in Atlanta. Doug Williams, the former Washington Redskin who quarterbacked one of Joe Gibbs's three Super Bowl champions, also was traveling and sought out Ward to introduce himself. That prompted Williams's later telephone call seeking Ward's assistance.

FSU's 1993 recruiting class included a running back from Baton Rouge, Louisiana, who was still mourning the murder of his mother. Betty Dunn Smothers, a policewoman who was providing security for a supermarket manager making a late-night bank deposit, was shot and killed in a robbery in January, during Warrick Dunn's senior season and in the midst of recruiting. Williams was acquainted with Dunn's mother. After Dunn decided to attend Florida State, Williams telephoned Ward and asked if Ward would take a personal interest in the freshman. Ward assured him that he would.

Later, "out of the clear blue," Williams related to *Palm Beach Post* reporter Scott Tolley, "Charlie called and asked, 'Do you think Warrick would want to room with me?'" That's how the senior who would win the Heisman Trophy and the freshman who became an invaluable contributor on a championship team launched a lasting friendship.

Ward has never betrayed the ideals his parents instilled in him. He has never been one to beat his chest and boast of accomplishments. (Charlie Ward Sr. and his wife, Willard, did not know that their son had been running for vice president of FSU's student body as a junior until they read in a newspaper that he had been elected.)

As the outpouring of accolades identifying him as college football's best and most dynamic player peaked, Ward continued to quietly deflect them. Actually, *quietly* doesn't accurately reflect his response. "His mother always told him to think before you speak," his father once told me. Nobody ever took that advice more to heart. A joint radio and talk-show appearance with Ward before the 1992 season amused Richt for weeks afterwards. "You know how nervous those guys are about dead-air time," he chuckled of the show's host. "I don't think Charlie answered a question. They'd be rephrasing the question by the time he had thought through his answer."

Speaking of his introspective superstar closer to the end of his FSU career, Richt said, "Charlie has his game plan for life, and he's not going to veer off of it. He's not one to run with the crowd. He's very strong in his faith, and he's going to do what he thinks is right by how he was brought up."

# C'mon Back and See Us

Chris Weinke, a three-sport star at Cretin-Durham High in St. Paul, Minnesota, first reported for football practice at Florida State in August 1990. Scouts and officials of baseball's Toronto Blue Jays followed in hot pursuit. They had invested a second-round draft pick in the slugging third baseman, and they had a deadline. If Weinke attended a single class at FSU, the Blue Jays would forfeit his rights. More pertinent, as history would reflect, as soon as Weinke attended a class, the five-year clock on his four years of college football eligibility would start ticking.

Weinke agonized over his decision. College football or pro baseball? Practicality tipped the scales. The desperate Blue Jays told Weinke they expected he'd be in the majors in three years. They didn't stop there. They upped the ante and offered a signing bonus of $375,000. Weinke chose baseball.

That made his next task a painful one. He had to notify Bobby Bowden. After watching Weinke in just a handful of practices, the coach already had told reporters, "He's better than I thought he'd be." And remember, on that same practice field were two talented but still unknown quantities—the eventual 1991 Heisman Trophy runner-up, Casey Weldon, and the 1993 Heisman winner, Charlie Ward.

Weinke knew he'd be disappointing Bowden, but he worried about infuriating him. Years later he still marveled at the reaction. "He was unbelievable," Weinke said. "He said he considered me one of his, wished me success in baseball, and told me, 'If you ever want to come back and play, there will be a scholarship waiting for you.'" Turns out Bowden meant it.

Six years later, Weinke's baseball career had stalled. In September 1996 the Blue Jays sent him to an instructional league in Florida, intent on making him a catcher. But more than proximity prompted Weinke to attend a Seminoles home game against Clemson. He stopped by to visit Bowden.

Word that he was considering a return to college to play football already was circulating. Weinke later related that he received five firm recruiting pitches, including one from Arizona. But if Bowden still wanted him, he wanted FSU. Three months after their meeting, Weinke enrolled in time for spring practice.

Weinke celebrated his twenty-fifth birthday before a 1997 season, during which he made only two token appearances in relief of senior Thad Busby. The backup to Busby was Dan Kendra, another celebrated high school quarterback of great promise. But a knee injury to Kendra during 1998 spring drills ceded the FSU starting job to Weinke a month after he turned twenty-six.

The aforementioned disastrous second start and 24–7 loss at North Carolina State left doubts about how long Weinke would hold the job. His 6 interceptions broke an ignominious FSU record previously held by Bill Cappleman and matched that ACC record for passing infamy. Weinke didn't spare himself in post-mortems that day. "A lot of people played bad, and I probably played the worst," he said. "I was overthrowing people by 10 feet."

Weinke also speculated that there would be "people who want to run me out of town" greeting him when he took the Doak Campbell Stadium field for his first home start a week later. Instead he received a warm reception that he would reward repeatedly in a career marked by only one loss in his next thirty-two starts.

Weinke passed for 241 yards and 3 touchdowns in the 62–13

rout of Duke. More important he didn't suffer an interception. In fact, Florida State loomed as a national championship contender at 8–1, and Weinke's string of passes without interception had reached a school-record 218 when a neck injury sabotaged his season and threatened his career.

Just before halftime against Virginia, defensive end Patrick Kerney hammered Weinke from his blind side and drove him toward the turf. The injury occurred when the helmet of another converging defender slammed into Weinke's shoulder. "I was already down and I was hit and my neck got jammed," he said afterwards. "I knew I was hurt pretty bad."

Weinke walked from the field under his own power but with his numbed right throwing arm held tightly against his body. He spotted backup Marcus Outzen. "He told me he couldn't feel his arm and 'you're going to have to go,'" Outzen said.

Neither knew then that Weinke's season was over. Nobody knew then how close he had come to suffering a paralyzing injury. Weinke was not hospitalized that night. But X-rays the next day revealed a herniated disk and a thumbnail-sized bone chip pressing against a nerve. "The more I heard [from doctors]," Bowden said later, "the more scary it got."

Weinke underwent surgery to fuse two vertebrae and to remove the herniated disk. But his suffering was just beginning. He was released from the hospital but readmitted within days when he was racked by nausea, dehydration, and excruciating headaches. A second surgery became necessary to correct a spinal fluid leak. He was left with a scar about 3 to 4 inches long in front of his neck and another from an 8-to-10-inch incision reaching from the back of his neck down between his shoulder blades.

*Chris Weinke directed the Seminoles to their perfect 1999 season, and the follow-ing year he won the Heisman Trophy.*

Before he was free of pain, he had lost more than twenty pounds off his statuesque frame. He still looked wan, even ghostly, some seven weeks later while watching the Seminoles prepare in Tempe, Arizona, for the Fiesta Bowl championship game against unbeaten Tennessee, a 23–16 loss in Outzen's third and final career start. Even then, if Weinke made a sudden move-ment, he became dizzy.

That's why a Weinke-centered cloud of doubt shadowed the Seminoles' prospects as they prepared for the 1999 season. Doctors had cleared him to play after extensive testing, and Weinke looked robust. But coaches did not subject him to contact in drills. A burden of proof remained. I remember writing before the opener against Louisiana Tech that the loudest ovation would not occur when Weinke trotted onto the field with the offense or when he drilled that first complete pass, but when he absorbed that first crushing tackle and got up to take the next snap.

Weinke didn't just pick up where he had left off. He propelled FSU to a perfect 12–0 season in which his poise and heroics under pressure helped the Seminoles survive upset bids by Georgia Tech, Miami, Clemson, Florida, and, in the Sugar Bowl showdown for the national championship, Virginia Tech.

After Michael Vick brought the Hokies back from a 28–7 deficit to a 29–28 lead and with the Seminoles reeling, Weinke restored his teammates' confidence by both word and deed in a climactic 18-point fourth quarter. He directed an eleven-play, 85-yard drive culminating in his 14-yard scoring pass to Ron Dugans as the Seminoles retook the lead, and he provided the finishing touch with a 43-yard touchdown strike to Peter Warrick.

Though Weinke had a year of eligibility remaining, conventional wisdom shouted that he would ride the wave of adulation befitting a perfect ending into a second career in professional sports. He would be twenty-eight before the 2000 season. Most NFL players were on the downside of their careers by that age. The later he began his quest, the less likely a franchise would be to invest a high draft choice in him.

But Weinke saw room for improvement and figured it would more likely result from another season at the college level than a year on some NFL team's bench. He'll never second-guess that

# Sub Became Super

Both initially and in hindsight, Florida State coaches' decision to switch quarterbacks midway through the 1990 season cannot be faulted. Casey Weldon, promoted from backup, flaunted a 15–0 record as a starter before a 17–16 loss to Miami in 1991 aborted a championship challenge.

Bobby Bowden pictured Weldon as a collegiate version of Joe Montana, and Weldon flashed skills sufficiently suggestive of the San Francisco 49ers great that he finished runner-up to Michigan wide receiver Desmond Howard in Heisman Trophy balloting as a senior.

The quarterback demoted to make room for Weldon, however, has not become a mere footnote to FSU football history. He's the one ex-Seminole who has quarterbacked a team to a Super Bowl championship.

Brad Johnson, ninth-round draft choice in 1992, continued to make NFL headlines in the fall of 2005 when he stepped in for injured Daunte Culpepper and rescued the Minnesota Vikings from what shaped up as one of the most embarrassing and debilitating seasons in pro football history.

Ironically, Johnson's strengths as a pro cost him the job at FSU, even though he had passed for 251 yards in his next-to-last start against a typically stout Miami defense. He managed a game well. He read defenses well and limited risk in his decisions. But coaches warmed more to the gambler's mentality and flair that Weldon had. Johnson tended to pass to a back swinging out of the backfield; Weldon surveyed downfield more, looking for the home-run play, and he had the mobility to buy time.

Johnson lined up number one the first six games in 1990 and started in place of a hobbled Weldon in a 40–15 victory at Louisville in 1991. Expressing his confidence in Johnson before the Louisville game, Bowden said, "More than a few NFL scouts who have come in and watched us practice have said they were interested in both our quarterbacks."

Though Johnson had to wait until the 227th selection in that 1992 draft, he defied the odds to become a starter at Minnesota, to reach the Pro Bowl as a Washington Redskin in 1999, and finally to provide a steady hand on the steering wheel in quarterbacking Jon Gruden's 2002 Tampa Bay Buccaneers to the NFL Super Bowl pinnacle.

*Quarterback Brad Johnson has had the most productive NFL career of any FSU quarterback, leading the Tampa Bay Buccaneers to a Super Bowl championship in 2003.*

As has become his habit, Johnson did all this without great fanfare but he did it with class. Then, as now, he was the antithesis of the me-first athlete, poles apart from the Terrell Owenses and Latrell Sprewells of the world.

I remember then-quarterbacks coach Mark Richt's admiration for Johnson. He described Johnson's demeanor in handling the disappointment of the quarterback change in a word: "Awesome." Richt's sister, Nikki, also had a positive reaction to Johnson. She married him.

decision, which resulted in his membership on a Heisman honor roll adorned by names like Felix Blanchard, Ernie Davis, Paul Hornung, Roger Staubach, Johnny Rodgers, Archie Griffin, Herschel Walker, Barry Sanders . . . and Charlie Ward.

Weinke's 2000 season was not without great disappointment. Though a foot injury limited him to only a few snaps in practice the week of the Miami game, he passed for 496 yards. But he also suffered two costly interceptions. And even after Weinke rallied the Seminoles from a 20–10 deficit to a 24–20 advantage in a frenzied final five minutes, University of Miami quarterback Ken Dorsey answered with a game-winning drive concluded by his 13-yard touchdown pass to tight end Jeremy Shockey with 46 seconds left. Naturally, Weinke drove FSU to within a 49-yard field-goal bid for a tie and overtime on the final play. But walk-on Matt Munyon sent the kick—all together now—"wide right."

Weinke also would exit on a losing note. He lost his leading receiver, Marvin "Snoop" Minnis, to academic misfeasance before the Orange Bowl. Whether Minnis would have made a difference is difficult to assess, because linebackers Rocky Calmus and Torrance Marshall helped Oklahoma paint a defensive masterpiece in the 13–2 slugfest that secured a 13–0 record and national championship for the Sooners.

The Orange Bowl had been trumpeted as a duel between Heisman Trophy winner Weinke and runner-up Josh Heupel of Oklahoma. FSU arrived averaging 42.4 points per game and Oklahoma with a 39-points-per-game average. But FSU's defense played almost as spectacularly as Oklahoma's. The game's lone touchdown didn't come until midway through the fourth quarter, and Oklahoma had to travel only 15 yards to get it after Weinke fumbled while scrambling in desperation out of a collapsing pocket. Heupel passed for 214 yards with 1 interception, Weinke for 274 yards but with 2 interceptions.

A concerted campaign in the national media had touted Heupel for the Heisman on the basis of Weinke's age. The premise was lame. Without fueling the yearly debate over the Heisman almost unfailingly going to a skill-position player on offense, Weinke's remarkable season was worthy of the top prize. The trauma he survived and overcame at the end of his 1998 season may have tipped the scales for some who wrestled with the age issue before casting ballots.

Weinke's family suffered with him during the weeks after his injury and his rehabilitation. I spoke to his mother, Betty, the week of the Heisman Trophy ceremonies, and she related a futile battle with her fears for the better part of a year extending into the 1999 season. She had watched her son wheeled into an operating room for spinal surgery. Doctors could diagnose that he had fully recovered and carried no more risk of a similar injury than any other player upon his return. But what possible assurances did she have? "It was horrible," she said in that telephone conversation. "I kept psyching myself [during the 1999 season], 'You need to enjoy more than you worry.' But for so long, those were just words."

She finally came to grips with her anxiety. "I knew I'd look back and would have missed out if I continued in the 'worry' state I was in the first few games after he came back."

What she would have missed was the full appreciation of a perfect season that brought Florida State a national championship and another that put her son's name on a trophy that promises immortality.

# Rugged Road to Glory

Bobby Bowden never has been one to duck a challenge. But neither is he a masochist. No coach with an ounce of sanity would have built the barriers to success that Clay Stapleton, Florida State University athletic director from April 1971 until February 1973, erected in a scheduling flurry that mortgaged a program's future. Presumably, Bowden didn't spend much time studying future schedules when he elected to leave West Virginia for FSU in 1976.

Sure he knew he had a steep climb ahead of him. FSU had won all of four times in the previous three years. But only after he was in place in Tallahassee did he digest the truly monumental task confronting him. Surveying the future long-term, he could draw only one conclusion: FSU might be overmatched.

Stapleton directed a second-tier athletic program without great resources. He was necessarily motivated by the healthy financial guarantees served up by traditional football powers in search of a home-field "opponent." The visitor walked away with a nice paycheck, the home team with a near-certain victory. Stapleton took this business approach to an extreme, however. He signed contracts for four games with Nebraska, five games with Louisiana State, two games with Ohio State, two games with Arizona State, and a single game with Notre Dame, none to take effect before the 1979 season.

The contracts had this in common: FSU would be the visiting team in every game. The Cornhuskers, Tigers, Buckeyes, Wildcats, and Fighting Irish would not be required to play in Tallahassee. You've heard of home-and-away contracts? These were away-and-away . . . or, in the deal with LSU, away-and-away-and-away-and-away-and-away.

The most blatant manifestation of this auction was a road trip from hell that Bowden would subsequently proclaim "Oktoberfest."

"I remember when I came here in 1976, I looked at that 1981 schedule and thought, 'You'd better be gone by then,'" Bowden reflected years later. What he saw was a potential coach-killer. The Seminoles would be required to hit the road for five consecutive games: at Nebraska, at Ohio State, at Notre Dame, at Pittsburgh, at Louisiana State. (The Steelers and Raiders apparently had no open dates.)

The asterisk here, and it should be in headline size, is that Bowden already had been dubbed King of the Road before that 1981 Oktoberfest. The 11–0 and 10–1 regular seasons of 1979 and 1980 featured two victories at LSU—one of which convinced Bowden to reject a job overture from LSU athletic director Paul Dietzel—and a memorable 18–14 victory over Nebraska that Bowden still ranks with his greatest.

But the 1981 Seminoles were in rebuilding mode, with a revamped defense no longer built around all-world nose tackle Ron Simmons and linebackers Paul Piurowski and Reggie Herring. That elevated the overall task to Herculean. Nebraska and Pittsburgh particularly had significant manpower advantages.

A homegrown Pittsburgh guy with a missile-launcher of a right arm riddled the Seminoles' secondary for 251 passing yards and 3 touchdowns in a 42–14 romp in game four of the punishing five-game gantlet. You've heard of him: Dan Marino.

Names of the standouts in a 34–14 Nebraska victory over the Seminoles also would appear in plenty of headlines over the next decade. Irving Fryar, whose 82-yard punt return broke open a 10–7 game, became the New England Patriots' and NFL's number one draft pick in 1984. Roger Craig's 94-yard touchdown escape contributed to a 234-yard rushing day; he went on to a productive career with the San Francisco 49ers that featured a 3-touchdown Super Bowl in a 38–16 cruise past the Dolphins in 1985. Mike Rozier, who netted 72 mop-up yards as Craig's backup in that 1981 romp, became a Heisman Trophy recipient after the 1983 season.

But the Seminoles emerged from Oktoberfest with three victories. True, Ohio State, Notre Dame, and Louisiana State were not at the peaks of their football prowess. Notre Dame's FSU test came five games into a five-year era of mediocrity that ranks the engaging and enthusiastic Gerry Faust with the least successful coaches in Golden Dome history. Louisiana State had slipped from the national stage but would return to top-twenty stature in six of the next seven seasons. And Ohio State still was searching for a post–Woody Hayes identity under Earle Bruce.

But compare Florida State tradition at that stage to the history that had been written at Ohio State, Notre Dame, and LSU. Invading such storied college football venues and emerging with victories spoke volumes. Besides, when all the AP votes were counted at year's end, Ohio State would rank number fifteen in the nation, and among the fourteen teams that outpolled them would be Pittsburgh at number four and Nebraska at number eleven.

After the loss at Nebraska and in the first actual October game, FSU ventured into the horseshoe stadium where a tuba player dots the "i" and fired the first of a double-barreled blast into Ohio State's reputation that no one else had achieved for nearly two decades.

The last school to win in visits to "The House That Woody Built" in consecutive seasons was Penn State in 1963 and 1964. The 1981 Seminoles overcame a 458-yard passing performance by Art Schlichter with second-half touchdown drives covering 88 and 99 yards as Rick Stockstill accumulated 299 passing yards of his own. This was not Woody Hayes's "3 yards and a cloud of dust" approach to offense. The next year, true to Bowden ingenuity, quarterback Kelly Lowrey passed for a touchdown, caught a pass for another, and ran for a third — off a faked field goal — in a 34–17 FSU triumph.

Back to Oktoberfest.

The 19–13 victory at Notre Dame especially enraptured Bowden. As a thirteen-year-old in Birmingham, Alabama, Bowden had been confined to bed with rheumatic fever for months. A radio provided periodic escape from the monotony and boredom. He became an admirer of Notre Dame football history while listening to broadcasts of the Irish's games early in the Frank Leahy era.

In Bowden's reminiscing about those days, the legends of Notre Dame 1940s lore would roll off his tongue dramatically, emphatically, syllable by syllable: Angelo Bertelli, Emil Sitko, Johnny Lujack, Leon Hart. He greatly anticipated the trip to South Bend, Indiana, and the chance to walk where those ghosts of greatness had run. "Notre Dame is Notre Dame," he'd say. "There are some great names in sports: the New York Yankees, the Boston Celtics . . . Notre Dame is one of those."

Stockstill's 5-yard touchdown pass to halfback Michael Whiting broke a 13–13 tie and staked the Seminoles to a victory that certainly was not an artistic success but provided Bowden a satisfaction that few would understand.

Travel through time thirteen years to the day-after euphoria produced by a 23–16 FSU triumph over Notre Dame in Orlando and weigh the words of an exultant Bowden: "It's been a long time since I've been as thrilled over a victory as I was yesterday. Notre Dame is the biggest name in college football. A win over Notre Dame at any time in any circumstances is good for your résumé."

Be reminded that not nine months earlier, FSU had finally given Bowden an overdue national championship against Nebraska in the Orange Bowl. But, hey, this was Notre Dame.

Next during Oktoberfest came Pittsburgh. All week there had been reports that Marino might not be able to play because of a sore shoulder. After the future Pro Football Hall of Famer reduced FSU's secondary to a shambles without evidence of an iota of pain, Bowden sat down for his postgame press conference, promptly poked a finger into his mouth, and tugged at his cheek, suggesting a fish on a hook.

FSU rolled on into Baton Rouge 4–2 on the season, 2–2 on tour, and with an opportunity to emerge with a third consecutive victory over the Tigers and a juiced-up fan base normally as raucous as any anywhere. Defensive tackle David Ponder observed the week of the game, "From what I hear, those fans can really put the heat on you. You think the world's caving in, the way people tell it. But they haven't had a whole lot to yell about in our games [in 1979 and 1980]."

Jimmy Jordan had passed for 312 yards and 3 touchdowns in a 24–19 victory in 1979 that included a meaningless late LSU touchdown. And the Seminoles launched their 1980 season with a 16–0 shutout in which there was precious little for fans to roar about after the pregame ritual in those days of rolling Mike the Tiger's cage around the field and prodding him to elicit a growl into a live microphone.

*Running back Greg Allen had two strong performances against a tough LSU team in 1981 and 1982.*

Again in 1981, FSU showed up with an antidote to ear-numbing noise. Freshman tailback Greg Allen sprinted 66 yards on the Seminoles' first offensive snap to set up a field goal, and before the first quarter had ended, Bowden's bunch had muted opposition with a 17–0 advantage that grew to 38–14. The final quarter played out before few witnesses wearing purple and gold.

The postscript to an ultimately successful Oktoberfest that enhanced FSU's growing reputation on the national stage was a homecoming 56–31 rout of Western Carolina to improve to 6–2 . . . and then a complete collapse. There was a toll to be paid. "We had nothing after that," Bowden said. "We battled a real good Miami team to the wire and then got stomped by Southern Mississippi and stomped by Florida."

Miami, in the midst of reconstruction under Howard Schnellenberger, took the final bit of steam out of the Seminoles as future Buffalo Bills great Jim Kelly directed a 27–19 victory. Reggie Collier, a dynamic twin threat as a passer and runner, then picked at the defense's carcass as Southern Mississippi scored on its first seven possessions in a 58–14 humiliation. Florida expanded a 13–3 halftime advantage to 35–3 against Seminoles looking for an escape hatch.

Tailback Ricky Williams concluded, "Everybody was so pumped up about Oktoberfest that when it ended, it was like the season ended. Everybody was tired and not really into it."

Center Tom McCormick seconded that emotion. "I guess everybody got burned out," he said. "When we should have come on strong, we sort of just dwindled out."

That became the final Bobby Bowden–coached team to fail to qualify for a bowl. But in retrospect, Stapleton's rampantly ambitious mission to raise FSU's national profile accomplished precisely that, and the toll Oktoberfest took on the 1981 Seminoles proved to be well worth the future rewards.

True, the next five seasons would find Florida State on the fringes of national contention and not quite ready for the prime-time exposure that became standard from 1987 forward. Three-loss seasons in 1982, 1984, and 1985 kept company with two four-loss campaigns in 1983 and 1986. But high points during that five-year span included a fourth victory in the five games at Louisiana State, a split in the second "away-and-away" deal with Nebraska, the second of those back-to-back victories at Ohio State, and a sweep of the drama-crammed trips to Arizona State.

In addition, the 1986 Florida State team traveled to Michigan for the first of two road games separated by five years in yet another one-sided deal. A furor over officiating by a split crew of Big Ten and Southern Independent striped shirts followed a 20–18 victory by Bo Schembechler's Wolverines. No such debate accompanied the sensational 51–31 victory engineered by quarterback Casey Weldon in 1991.

The single loss at LSU came in a showdown for an Orange Bowl invitation in 1982 and aroused the rabid emotions that Tigers fans had been unable to unleash in the other four FSU visits.

"Yeah, I remember that one," Bowden said a couple seasons later. "That was about as nasty as it can get, and not just from the noise, which was greater than anywhere else I can remember. They were throwing oranges all over the place; they finally got a 15-yard penalty, I think, when one hit an official. And then, late in that game, that fog rolled in off the Mississippi River, and you couldn't see." The scene was eerie.

# Calling All QBs

Two games don't form a pattern. But Florida State's trips to Tempe, Arizona, to play Arizona State in 1983 and 1984 had enough in common to start a positive though abbreviated trend should the series ever resume. Both games were thrillers, and both created a career highlight for a Seminole who hadn't planned to leave the bench.

"[Arizona State] seems to bring out the best in our second-string quarterbacks," coach Bobby Bowden said after a gut-wrenching 52–44 survival in 1984, despite the most prolific passing performance by an opposing quarterback in FSU football history.

Jeff Van Raaphorst shredded the Seminoles' secondary for 532 passing yards and 4 touchdowns, but a frenzied fourth-quarter rally by the Sun Devils fell short because Kirk Coker played the game of his life off the bench.

Coker inherited a 20–10 deficit when starting quarterback Eric Thomas limped off with a severe hip pointer late in the first half. No, he didn't become a one-man wrecking crew. But his touchdown passes to Jessie Hester on plays covering 28 and 69 yards complemented tailback Greg Allen's 223 rushing yards (including an 81-yard touchdown escape) and Joe Wessel's 2 touchdowns off punt blocks as FSU established a lead even Van Raaphorst couldn't erase.

"Our other trips there, we kind of took the crowd out of it by getting ahead of them," Bowden said. But not that bizarre 1982 night. Freshman tailback Dalton Hilliard's dancing feet carried him to 183 yards and 4 touchdowns in a 55–21 romp that sent LSU to Miami for a 21–20 Orange Bowl loss to Nebraska.

A happy and relieved Coker admitted afterwards, "When I saw Eric motion over to the sideline that he couldn't throw the ball because his hip hurt so bad, my heart fell right down into my shoes." If so, he concealed his jitters admirably from his teammates and ASU defenders. He had previously attempted one pass in his career; it was incomplete. But on his first snap against the Sun Devils, he hooked up with receiver Hassan Jones for 45 yards. So much for nerves.

Hester took a particular liking to Tempe. His role in a 29–26 victory the year before was even more memorable and dramatic. He caught a 10-yard pass for the winning touchdown with 6 seconds remaining to climax a ten-play drive that covered 82 yards in precisely 82 seconds.

The catalyst, Bob Davis, came off FSU's bench when starting quarterback Kelly Lowrey sprained a knee late in the third quarter. Davis completed 8 of 12 passes for 104 yards directing two fourth-quarter touchdown drives. Just as critical as his touchdown strike to Hester capping the second was the fourth-down-and-five pass to tight end Tom Wheeler for a 16-yard pickup that set everything in motion.

Davis later said he didn't quite know how to react to all the plaudits and press. "Before, I was pretty much unheard of," he said, smiling.

Florida State's second victory at Nebraska, 17–13 two games into the 9–3 season of 1985, is as memorable for playing conditions as the fog-bound 1982 loss at LSU. Debilitating, blast-furnace heat had harsh effects not only on the field but also in the stands. According to local newspaper accounts the next day, three first-aid-station assistants suffered heat exhaustion from hauling fans from the stands on stretchers. Concessionaires started with eighty thousand pounds of ice but ran out long before the end of the game. The temperature on the All-Pro turf was measured at 133 degrees; at shoulder height it measured 103 degrees.

But FSU defenders played as if they had sold their souls to the devil. Nebraska fullback Tom Rathman bolted 60 yards for a touchdown in the game's first two minutes. But sophomore line-backer Paul McGowan, who in 1987 became the first recipient of the Butkus Award, operated at the hub of a bend-don't-break effort through a scoreless second half that had offensive players chanting "Dee-fense! Dee-fense!" in a victorious locker room.

Typically, the Huskers tried to wear down and demoralize Seminole defenders with a bruising rushing game that produced 372 yards. But they couldn't crack the FSU goal line after Doug DuBose's 1-yard touchdown produced a 13–10 lead midway through the second quarter.

McGowan, the son of a career navy man who served on a nuclear-powered sub, himself continually submarined Husker ballcarriers. He was credited with fourteen tackles. But the clincher came on his midfield interception of a pass by quarter-back McCathorn Clayton shortly after McGowan and mates had rendered fourth-quarter Nebraska drives to first downs at FSU's 14 yard line and 13 yard line pointless.

Safety Stan Shiver recovered a Rathman fumble to spoil the first; huge plays by McGowan and Shiver preceded an errant field-goal attempt on the second. That defense had so many heroes that day. I remember tight end Gaylon White interrupting reporters' questions to Gerald Nichols to reach through them and tell the future New York Jets nose tackle, "I want to shake your hand."

One other lingering memory from that steamy day is the class of Nebraska fans whose mid-America values always seemed to keep football in perspective. As a perspiring but joyous Bowden trotted toward the dressing room after the game, red-clad fans in that corner of the stadium stood and applauded him and the Seminoles. Some reached to shake Bowden's hand.

*Bobby Bowden and Nebraska coach Tom Osborne shake hands amidst a swarm of media after FSU's dramatic 18–16 Orange Bowl victory for the 1993 national title.*

I've always felt that class evolved from the professorial Tom Osborne, who for so long epitomized the best of college athletics. His twenty-five seasons as Huskers head coach after he succeeded mentor Bob Devaney produced 255 victories, and he followed his coaching career by getting elected to the U.S. House of Representatives by landslide margins.

Those home-grown plowboys who lined up from tackle to tackle and mashed everybody who got in their blocking lanes so that Osborne's I-backs could run wild didn't mind bruising you. But in every other way, Osborne always seemed the gracious host to Bowden, his staff, and his players.

Speaking of that unending parade of productive I-backs brings to mind a Bowden comment before FSU's 1986 return to Lincoln and the 34–17 loss that concluded Stapleton's four-year deal. DuBose, who had rushed for 129 yards against the Seminoles in that sauna the year before, already had been lost for the season with a knee injury, and Bowden didn't know much about who had replaced him. "But whoever is back there will make All-Big Eight," he quipped.

Here's a quick review of Stapleton's legacy:

- Four games at Nebraska: FSU 2–2
- Five games at Louisiana State: FSU 4–1
- Two games at Ohio State: FSU 2–0
- Two games at Arizona State: FSU 2–0
- One game at Notre Dame: FSU 1–0

The math is simple: eleven victories, three losses. Lingering impact on the national psyche: Bobby Bowden and Florida State would go anywhere to play anybody.

The great *Los Angeles Times* sports columnist Jim Murray once wrote of Bear Bryant's marvelous Alabama dynasty that it was difficult to tell whether the favorably scheduled Tide was slaying dragons or kicking over baby carriages. Florida State made its reputation slaying dragons.

# The Seminoles Before Bobby

Lee Corso, whose rabid cheerleading for college football matches fellow ESPN analyst Dick Vitale's for college basketball, strolled through downtown Tempe, Arizona, on a December 1998 morning and reminisced about a benchmark in Florida State history. Bobby Bowden's Seminoles were preparing to play in their third national-championship game in six seasons in the Fiesta Bowl several nights later. They would square off against unbeaten Southeastern Conference champion Tennessee. But Corso was reflecting on an FSU-Tennessee meeting forty years earlier. "I think that 10–0 win over Tennessee in Knoxville in 1958 was the biggest game in Florida State football," he said.

He had a viable case. That was at a time when coach Tom Nugent, in his sixth but final season at FSU before he moved on to Maryland, was still trying to get the eleven-year-old football program out from under a giant shadow. FSU had been an all-girls school until May 1947, a lingering subject of some levity and needling.

From a 0–5 debut under Ed Williamson, who assembled a team in mere months for the 1947 season, FSU had progressed from playing Cumberland and Erskine and Millsaps in the late 1940s to Miami and Louisville and North Carolina State before Nugent took command in 1953. Don Veller had significantly upgraded FSU football in his 31–12–1 tenure, but the mountain to be climbed remained steep.

In spite of an early hammerlock on a tame N.C. State in the early 1950s, FSU stood 0–14 against more established programs at Auburn, Georgia, Miami, and Georgia Tech midway through the 1958 season as the Seminoles prepared to play Bowden Wyatt's Volunteers in Knoxville.

It's not as if the Seminoles needed greater motivation, said Corso, then a twenty-three-year-old coach of FSU's defensive backs. But the emotions may have been running a little higher, from Nugent on down, because of a remark by Wyatt at a coaching clinic.

"Coach Nugent was the most innovative guy that coaching had seen in years," Corso said. "He was way ahead of his time. We ran the 'shifty I' in 1953, a hell of a long time before anyone came up with all these shifting offenses with backs out of the backfield . . . That wasn't done then."

Nugent conducted a clinic called "passing fancy" at FSU, and Wyatt attended. Corso remembered the pride Nugent took in the meticulously manicured playing field. Whether or not Wyatt intended a slight, Corso recalled, "He said, 'We don't grow beautiful grass at Tennessee. We just teach great football.'"

If that's not the first time Corso said, "Not so fast, my friend," it should have been. FSU put a stranglehold on Tennessee in the 10–0 shutout that Corso described as "monumental . . . earth-shaking." Halfback Fred Pickard carried 22 times for 133 yards, and that was 22 more yards than the Vols' offense produced.

"That was the first win over a Southeastern Conference team," said Corso, "the first over a program people recognized as a major power. After that, we had legitimacy in the South." The victory warranted the heroes' welcome an estimated three thousand FSU fans gave the Seminoles upon their return to Tallahassee.

Incidentally, the game was supposed to match FSU quarterback Joe Majors against his brother Billy, long-time *Tallahassee Democrat* sports columnist Bill McGrotha wrote in his fact-filled book *Seminoles! The First 40 Years*. Yes, both are from the famed Majors clan, Tennessee football's First Family. But Billy suffered an injury in the first quarter.

Two weeks later, Nugent's troops finally achieved their first

Lee Corso, recognized today for his college football coverage on ESPN, played his college ball at FSU.

victory over Miami, 17–6, with the help of an interception and a 42-yard touchdown return by Joe Majors. But as gratifying as that was, it only set the stage for a subsequent 21–7 loss that represented a significant off-field victory. FSU finally got a chance to line up against the University of Florida.

Threatened action by the Florida legislature and apparent well-timed remarks by Governor LeRoy Collins, who did not consider a football series a legislative matter, finally prompted the presidents of the two universities to arrange for the University of Florida to schedule, with great reluctance, the erstwhile Florida State College for Women.

That 1958 kickoff came too late for Corso the player, who in 1953 became arguably the most consequential recruit in FSU's neophyte football history. He had been a three-sport star at Miami Jackson High, and Nugent persuaded him to become a Seminole with a couple of recruiting promises. "At that time," Corso said, "I was thinking about signing with the Brooklyn Dodgers organization for $15,000. That was a lot of money back then. But Coach Nugent gave me an opportunity to play football without it interfering with my baseball." During spring football drills, Corso was playing shortstop on another field.

Nugent also promised Corso he could start at quarterback the first game of his freshman season. He did, in front of friends, family, and former classmates in Miami's Orange Bowl. That didn't turn out so well. FSU lost, 27–0.

But before Corso's FSU career ended, he had led the team in rushing in 1955 with 431 yards, led it in passing in 1956 with a modest 369 yards and 5 touchdown passes and, in the era before two-platoon football, intercepted 14 passes in his career. That stood as an FSU record until Monk Bonasorte broke it almost a quarter-century later. Even today, only three players have as many or more than Corso's 14 pass thefts. Terrell Buckley buried Bonasorte's record with 21. Corso still shares third place in the FSU record book with (drum roll) Deion Sanders. Yo!

That initial Florida-FSU agreement was lopsided. One notable provision: The first six games in the series would be played in Gainesville. It should not come as a startling revelation that FSU did not beat Florida until the first time the Gators had to visit Tallahassee.

In the meantime, after Nugent's six seasons and a 1959 head-coaching cameo by Perry Moss, FSU once again had imported an imaginative head coach who believed in a wide-open, crowd-pleasing passing game. Bill Peterson earned his reputation with game plans that showcased FSU's great passing combinations of the 1960s: Steve Tensi to Fred Biletnikoff; and Gary Pajcic, Kim Hammond, and Bill Cappelman to Ron Sellers.

But some who might otherwise have appreciated his strategic expertise probably got caught up in the mangled syntax and never-ending malapropisms that made Peterson not only a comical figure but also a lovable one. I was one of the "sport" writers who covered his 1969 and 1970 teams, and I have no doubt that he often intentionally transposed words to amuse and/or baffle the writers. If his eyes had a little twinkle when he said something like "let sleeping bags lie," you could safely assume he was poking fun at himself so you could share a laugh together.

As I wrote an obituary column on Peterson in August 1993, I was wishing I had had the foresight to note every occasion of his oratorical butchery. I hadn't. But McGrotha, the ultimate FSU football historian until his death, documented the ones that made the greatest impression on him. I freely borrowed and attributed them in that column.

I chuckled at the Peterson admonishment, "Don't kill the goose that lays the deviled egg." And at the time he began a postgame prayer, "Now I lay me down to sleep," realized his miscue, and quickly lateraled the prayer duty to a player. But I

*Coach Bill Peterson (front row, center) poses with his staff, which included a young Bobby Bowden (front row, far left).*

laughed out loud at McGrotha's quoting from Peterson's David-and-Goliath motivational battle cry to an outmanned FSU team:

"David needed some help, and he went out and got this sling and some rocks, and he practiced. Just like you guys, he didn't like to practice, but he kept at it. David just went out there and practiced and practiced and practiced, slinging those rocks at tin cans and old beer bottles for days and days and days." Rolling Rock?

But if you think he confused only sportswriters, you would have learned better had you been on sidelines across from him and tried to decipher what he was doing on offense. An ABC-TV documentary clip that included scenes from one of Florida State's games documented one storied coach's bafflement. "What's going on out there?" bellowed an exasperated Paul "Bear" Bryant in the midst of upstart Florida State's 37–37 tie with the Bear's 1967 Alabama Crimson Tide. "What the *hell* is going on out there?"

Before Peterson departed to become both coach and athletic director at Rice in 1971, he had coached the Seminoles to sixty-two victories and eleven ties in 115 games over eleven seasons. That FSU flaunted one of the nation's most impressive passing attacks under "Coach Pete" is verifiable by the consensus All-America honors accorded Biletnikoff and Sellers.

In retrospect, however, Peterson's greatest attribute may not have been in the Xs-and-Os blueprint of a passing scheme but in his ability to spot and assess coaching talent. "He's one of the best I've ever seen at hiring the right people," one former aide said.

Peterson's FSU staffs included Bill Parcells and Joe Gibbs, who went on to coach four Super Bowl championship teams between them, plus a third future NFL head coach, Dan Henning. Eventual college head coaches like Don James (Washington), Vince Gibson (Kansas State), and John Coatta (Wisconsin) also learned under Pete at FSU.

I haven't yet mentioned the aide who marveled at Peterson's ability to hire young coaches and help them develop. A fellow named Bobby Bowden. Peterson had to credit Gibson for the importation of Bowden, who was then head coach at Howard College (now Samford) in Birmingham. Bowden and Gibson had grown up together there.

"The church was sort of the center of activity," Bowden said of his teenage years. "I lived about 3 blocks from the church, [future wife] Ann a block to the other side, and Vince 3 blocks to that side. I knew Vince before I knew Ann. Because he was a little younger, I was kind of Vince's hero."

Bowden attended Alabama for a semester but transferred to Howard after he and Ann married (he was nineteen, Ann sixteen). There, Bowden and Gibson were teammates for two seasons. "I think one time I hit him with 3 touchdown passes," Bowden recalled. "He transferred to Florida State after I graduated [in 1953]."

Bowden landed a job as head coach at South Georgia Junior College in 1956, and he hired Gibson. They were together there for three years. (It was in 1958 that Bowden's team lost to a Florida State freshman team coached by—Hel-lo!—Lee Corso.) But South Georgia dropped football, Gibson became a graduate assistant at Florida State, and Bowden returned to his alma mater as head coach from 1959 through 1962. "Vince and I always stayed in contact, and he's the one who told Peterson he needed to hire me," Bowden said.

# No Fashion Plate, but Great

No offense was intended when, the day after Super Bowl XI, I wrote that the Most Valuable Player in the Oakland Raiders' 32–14 romp past Minnesota didn't win the award "on his looks." Fred Biletnikoff cut neither an imposing nor a dashing figure.

Florida State University's first consensus All-American capped a brilliant college career by catching 4 touchdown passes in a 36–19 Gator Bowl victory over Oklahoma in January 1965. Before leaving the field, under the goalposts, he signed a contract to play for Al Davis's Raiders in the midst of the fledgling American Football League's pre-merger war for talent with the established National Football League.

Davis presented Biletnikoff for induction into the Pro Football Hall of Fame twenty-three and a half years later and took note of number 25's less-than-stylish appearance in uniform. "His loose sleeves, his socks hanging down, his eyes blackened, the stick-um on his fingers . . . genius comes in many different configurations," Davis said at the ceremony. The thinning, dirty-blond hair that hung damply and limply down to his neck when Biletnikoff would take off his helmet added an exclamation point to his raggedy appearance.

But the star quality so evident as Biletnikoff and quarterback Steve Tensi helped introduce Coach Bill Peterson's style of football to the nation in the early 1960s blossomed even more in a fourteen-year professional career.

Super Bowl XI showcased his talents and provided a career peak. Three of his four pass receptions from Ken Stabler set up touchdowns, including a 48-yard gain to the Vikings' 2 yard line and a 17-yard grab to the 1 yard line.

Minnesota cornerback Nate Wright best captured Biletnikoff's ability after that game when he said, "He catches everything catchable and some passes that aren't . . . I've never played a man with his combination of moves and catching ability."

It was FSU's and Peterson's great fortune that shortly after Biletnikoff

*Fred Biletnikoff capped his FSU career by snaring four touchdown passes in the Gator Bowl.*

departed, Ron Sellers arrived. The lanky receiver nicknamed "Jingle Joints" proceeded to become the most prolific receiver in FSU history and, to this day, owns the records for most career catches (212) and yards receiving (3,598). He played five seasons in the NFL.

Like Biletnikoff, Sellers's FSU jersey number has been retired. And like Biletnikoff, he became a member of the College Football Hall of Fame.

That's how Bowden happened to be coaching future pro football great Biletnikoff and FSU's other receivers from 1963 through 1965. "Fred had to play defense, too," Bowden said. "I remember in 1963 we beat Miami [24–0]. Fred intercepted a pass by George Mira and ran 99 yards for a touchdown in that game."

Noteworthy is that when Biletnikoff graduated, Bowden turned to a sophomore named T. K. Wetherell to help fill the void. Like Joe Paterno at Penn State, Bowden will never lack for job security. He'll retire when he wants. But if he needed a friend in the court of opinion, he has one. Wetherell now is president of Florida State University.

Bowden, famous for his wit on the banquet and booster clubs circuit, has allowed one apocryphal story in which he incorporated popular president Bernie Sliger to live on through Wetherell. The original version went like this: The Seminoles are checking into the hotel for a bowl week, and tailback Sammie Smith has brought a stereo along with his luggage. Bowden calls over to President Sliger, "Hey, Doc, why don't you help Sammie with his bags?" And Dr. Sliger answers back, "I can't. I've got Deion's."

Undoubtedly Peterson's greatest victory at FSU—and Bowden's as an assistant there—had to be the Seminoles' breakthrough against Florida in 1964, though FSU had scrapped to a 3–3 tie in 1961. Memorably the slogan affixed to Florida players' helmets during practice the week of the game was, "Never, FSU, Never!"

Detailed in McGrotha's book is Florida coach Ray Graves's decision to start senior quarterback Tommy Shannon over a less-experienced sophomore and an early fumbled center-quarterback exchange forced by FSU linebacker Jack Shinholser at the Seminoles' 1 yard line. The outcome, many believe, hinged on that play, though the Gators wound up turning the ball over six times.

Tensi and Biletnikoff subsequently connected on a 55-yard touchdown play that staked FSU to a 7–0 lead, and Grant Murdock's third second-half field goal provided the final 16–7 cushion. Graves did turn to his sophomore quarterback in hopes of a rally, and Steve Spurrier did direct Florida's touchdown drive. But this was FSU's day.

Bowden had departed to become offensive coordinator at West Virginia before the 1966 season that produced the most contentious debate to this date among old-time Gators and Seminoles. Spurrier, three games into what became a Heisman Trophy–winning senior season, had directed Florida to a 22–19 lead, but, with only 28 seconds remaining, Gary Pajcic launched a 45-yard pass into the end zone to tight end Lane Fenner. Photographs in the *Tallahassee Democrat* the next morning showed Fenner in-bounds with apparent control of the football. A field judge who will live in infamy at FSU, Doug Moseley, ruled that Fenner juggled the ball going out of bounds. No catch. No touchdown. Florida victory.

In a takeout story on the Florida-FSU rivalry in 1991, I had a telephone interview with Wetherell, then the speaker of the Florida House of Representatives. He was in the pass pattern when Pajcic targeted Fenner. "There's no damned doubt [Fenner made the catch]," he insisted. A bit tongue-in-cheek, he added, "I don't mind them stealing it. I just wish they'd admit it."

According to Julian Clarkson, author of the book *Let No Man Put Asunder*, from which McGrotha quoted, one former Gator student did admit it. The gleeful ex-Gator allegedly needled an FSU fan, "You're right. He was in [bounds], and we stole

Ron Sellers, focal point of FSU's pass-happy offenses of the mid-1960s, still owns the school's records for receptions and receiving yards.

it from you. That makes it even sweeter." I tried to contact then-Governor Lawton Chiles to verify the quote attributed to him for my story, but he had left town for the Thanksgiving holiday. Wetherell said he had seen that quote. He said, "I'm surprised they didn't use that against him in the [gubernatorial] campaign. Somebody ought to have gone out to the game and handed out fliers with that on it. It would have cost him 100,000 votes."

When Peterson departed to become both coach and athletic director at Rice, one potential candidate to replace him was the young coach who had brought Louisville into town for the 1970 season opener and thrown a 9–7 scare into Peterson's final FSU team. His 8–3 Cardinals were preparing for a Pasadena Bowl appearance against Long Beach State in California when Corso got a telephone call from longtime FSU trainer Don Fauls. "Don said, 'The head coaching job's going to open. Are you interested?'" Corso related.

Corso discussed whether to pursue the job with his wife, Betsy. "But I'd given my word to the University of Louisville that if they'd give this young whippersnapper a chance, I wouldn't leave," at least until his program got a foothold. (It was two years later, after a 9–1 Louisville team had earned a share of the Missouri Valley Conference championship, that Indiana hired Corso away.)

You have to wonder how history would have been altered if Corso had applied for and won the job. Instead, former University of Tennessee assistant Larry Jones produced winning teams in 1971 and 1972 before a storm-tossed 0–11 collapse in 1973, and replacement Darrell Mudra's two seasons resulted in only four victories.

You also have to wonder what would have happened if another young coach, who did interview for the vacancy Peterson created, had been hired at that time. Bobby Bowden, who had just coached West Virginia to an 8–3 record in his first season after replacing Jim Carlen, didn't get the FSU job then. But he did five years later.

# Cornerback U.

Several days before University of Miami quarterback Vinny Testaverde accepted the 1986 Heisman Trophy, he sat for a question-and-answer session designed to flesh out his personality: What was his biggest thrill? The funniest moment in his career? His favorite singer? Who would he like to meet? That sort of stuff. But the question that elicited possibly his most unequivocal response related to football and the best defensive back he had challenged. "That number 2 from Florida State," he said.

Surely that's the last time somebody needed a jersey number to identify Deion Sanders. True, he hadn't adopted his prime-time persona yet, but even as a sophomore, he had begun to strut and preen in a national spotlight that glowed megawatts not just for the next two seasons but for the next two decades.

Even before Deion's freshman season had run its course, Bobby Bowden compared him to Bobby Butler. Arguably the greatest cornerback to have played at FSU to that point, Butler was five seasons into a twelve-year NFL career in Atlanta at the time. But it hardly required Bowden's keen eye for potential greatness to see that in Sanders.

Drawing on rhyme, a distinctive spelling of his first name, and Sanders's inescapable flair, I had begun a 1986 late-season feature, "That's Deion as in Neon," and suggested that the number on his jersey should by outlined by the twinkling lights that dash around a Las Vegas marquee.

Testaverde's endorsement preceded 1987 and 1988 seasons in which Sanders made every All-America team you could find. As a senior, he won the Jim Thorpe Award that honors college football's best defensive back. That was appropriate. When the Walter Camp Foundation selected its All-Century football team in 1999, Sanders got the nod as one cornerback. Another was Carlisle College's Jim Thorpe.

Sanders would have made headlines with his out-of-this-world skills if he had been struck mute as a child. But his talent was matched by his flamboyance. He was as lightning quick spouting one-liners as he was switching into high gear to blanket a receiver and defend a pass. And always, *always*, he played to the spotlight. He knew the value of showmanship.

Ronald Lewis caught the 18-yard touchdown pass from Danny McManus that staked the 1987 Seminoles to a 31–28 Fiesta Bowl victory over Nebraska, but Lewis refrained from any end-zone theatrics. He didn't milk the moment. He happily allowed himself to be swallowed up in his teammates' celebration. Speaking months later of his reluctance to self-promote in a moment of glory, Lewis said, "It's not my nature to showboat." He laughed and added, "Deion told me one time that if I wasn't careful, I'd 'humble' myself right out of the first round [of the NFL draft]."

*"Neon Deion" Sanders lit the FSU football firmament in the late 1980s.*

# Hardly a Perfect Science, But . . .

Look back five years later at any recruiting class at any major college and the challenge of correctly assessing talent in growing and maturing seventeen-year-olds will be painfully evident. Coaches recognize that recruiting is far from a perfect science.

That said, Florida State's consistently stingy defenses from the mid-1980s through a 2000 season that climaxed a string of fourteen straight years marked by ten or more victories relied mightily on a succession of All-America cornerbacks starting with Deion Sanders.

This was a snowball rolling downhill. Success breeds success. By 1990, high school stars could perceive a causal relationship: A) Martin Mayhew, Deion Sanders, and LeRoy Butler all played cornerback for Mickey Andrews; B) Mayhew and Sanders already were making their mark in the NFL, and Butler had just been drafted in the second round by Green Bay; therefore C) play cornerback for Mickey Andrews at Florida State, and an NFL career beckons.

Here's what Max Emfinger, prominent among assayers of high school talent, concluded after the 1990 recruiting wars: "Imagine that. The Southeastern Conference got none of the five top cornerbacks. The [now-defunct] Southwest Conference got none. Florida State got three."

He was speaking of Clifton Abraham, Corey Sawyer, and Corey Fuller. Twice the Associated Press recognized Sawyer as a second-team All-American. Abraham made first-team All-American in 1994. All three played in the NFL, Fuller enjoying a longer career than his more acclaimed teammates. All three more than satisfied the talent perceived in their high school years.

Samari Rolle, who followed, did not achieve All-America stature, but he also proceeded to an NFL career and played in the 2000 Pro Bowl.

Evident in a discussion with Andrews about the parade of talented defensive backs he has molded, FSU coaches have always thought outside the box in the search for high school players who might develop into top-flight college cornerbacks. It's not entirely a coincidence that Sanders, Sawyer, and Rolle all played quarterback in high school.

To catch a pass thief . . .

That's about the only way the words *humble* and *Deion* fit into the same sentence. He knew he was great. But what so greatly impressed FSU defensive coordinator Mickey Andrews is that Sanders never stopped trying to get better. "He's a cocky guy," Andrews said. "I've never coached one like him . . . I've never had one with the pure raw ability Deion has and yet has the work habits he does."

Sanders became Pied Piper to a parade of All-Americans who for much of a decade made FSU "Cornerback U." LeRoy Butler, who proceeded to a fourteen-year career with the Green Bay Packers, shifted from safety to corner in 1989 and made the Associated Press's All-America first team. Terrell Buckley, "T-Buck," set FSU single-season and career records for pass interceptions, making second-team AP All-American in 1990 and first team in 1991. Along came Corey Sawyer, selected to the second team in both 1992 and 1993, and Clifton Abraham, first team in 1994.

All will admit that they owe much of what they achieved at FSU and then in the NFL to Andrews, who chided, cajoled, and coaxed from them the best they had to offer. An old-school coach who played for Paul "Bear" Bryant at Alabama in the early 1960s, Andrews in 1996 became the inaugural winner of the Frank Broyles Award recognizing the top assistant in college coaching ranks.

Andrews routinely announces his displeasure over misplays on the practice field with a raspy, grating roar as he charges at the offender. But his humor-edged barbs often force the recipient of his wrath to stifle a smile.

Linebacker Daryl Bush got juked right off his feet by an incoming freshman running back during a 1993 preseason practice. (Others would learn quickly how difficult it was to tackle War-rick Dunn.) "I dove and tried to get ahold of the guy's ankles," a grinning Bush related later. "Coach Andrews ran up to me and said he thought Florida State had a diving team if I wanted him to try to get me on it."

Andrews has been known to walk up to one of his charges, throw an arm over his shoulders, and say in mock sadness, "I feel terrible. I owe your mother an apology. I told her I thought you could play football."

And the instruction never stops. Freshman cornerback James Colzie made a critical interception against Florida in the 33–21 vic-tory that sent FSU on to its 1993 national-championship showdown against Nebraska in the Orange Bowl. It was the first of his career. "I came off to the sideline," Colzie recalled, "and the first thing Coach Andrews told me was that I was in the wrong alignment. It didn't bother me at all. I *was* in the wrong alignment."

Few if any coaches delve deeper into the minutiae of tech-nique than Andrews. He traces that to his playing career at Alabama. "I wasn't a great player in high school and college," he said. "I didn't have great ability. I didn't have great speed. I had to pay attention to the little things. I had to be a detail-focused player, and then I had to play hard.

"I don't care how much talent you've got, you can never get too fast. You can never get too strong. You can never get too good. If a guy has great talent, it's my job to help him be a great player. That's some of the hardest coaching."

That means he drives the most talented players to seek per-fection. Nobody ever got closer, of course, than Sanders, who raised the bar impossibly high for all who followed.

# Prime Time

Deion Sanders saw himself not only as a prime-time performer but as an entertainer, too. He warmed to the spotlight. He craved the attention. And because he was so gregarious and loquacious, so comfortable center stage, he didn't have to work hard to get it.

Rob Wilson, FSU's sports information director, recalled a game at South Carolina late in Deion's senior season. Fans behind FSU's bench began by heckling the Seminoles, especially their All-America cornerback. They ended up laughing at his antics. FSU won, 59–0. And Wilson recalls Sanders standing on the bench late in the game, back to the field, and urging the Gamecocks' fans to go and demand their money back after witnessing such a lame performance.

Deion—as recognizable by a single name as "Tiger" or "Cher" or "Shaq"—also knew he had great wealth in his future. I can remember interviewing him in his dormitory room and being fascinated by a bulky gold medallion hanging around his neck. It was a circled dollar sign. That perceived security did cause a passing cloud of controversy over the close of his career. He gave academics cavalier treatment in his final semester. That eventually resulted in the "Deion rule," which stipulated that football players must take all their final exams in December or they would not be allowed to play in the postseason bowl.

In defense, Sanders told reporters that what they didn't understand is that he already had a winning lottery ticket (his rare talent) but had not cashed it yet. "Everybody knows I'm going to be a millionaire," he said on another occasion. "That's not a secret."

Mickey Andrews, FSU's defensive coordinator for more than two decades, has been the Pied Piper for a parade of All-America cornerbacks.

Sanders identified with a college rival who subsequently became both a pro rival and teammate. He once said, "Every time I touch that ball [on an interception or returning a punt], I'm looking for that end zone." Then he elaborated, "I heard Michael Irvin say one time, 'Every time I get the ball, all I see in the end zone is money.'"

That infatuation with the riches he was sure would follow his college career provided a somewhat recurring theme. Against Michigan State his senior season, Sanders suffered a knee injury that forced him to miss the next two games. He fleetingly feared the worst. "I was scared to death," he admitted after doctors assured him he had suffered only a moderate sprain. "My whole life, my career, flashed in front of me . . . I saw dollar signs jumping back across the fence, away from me."

But Sanders reaped monetary rewards not only in football but also in baseball. In addition to establishing himself as a perennial all-pro after the Atlanta Falcons made him the fifth pick in the 1989 NFL draft, Sanders "moonlighted" in baseball. He reached the majors and played center field for the Atlanta Braves and Cincinnati Reds.

Football, however, was the more natural fit for his flamboyance. He playfully speculated before his senior season at FSU that he'd have made an even bigger splash at the University of Miami where, he suggested, Jimmy Johnson had looser reins and players were allowed to be a bit more free-spirited. "The Miami players are more 'me,'" he said. "Michael Irvin's the flashy type; he wears the jewelry like I do. [Safety] Bennie Blades talking and intimidating out there on the field . . . same thing I do. They did what they wanted out there.

"Don't get me wrong. I love it here at Florida State. I wouldn't trade my years here for anything. We're a great team, and Coach Bowden is a great coach. But we stress composure. We aren't totally restrained, but . . .

"Coach Bowden lets me do a little more than he would like me to, but I try not to take it too far. I'm no Bosworth," he said, referencing the occasionally outrageous Oklahoma linebacker Brian Bosworth.

Still, Sanders loved the on-field banter with opponents. "I'm coming up to the line talking: 'C'mon, baby, it's you and me all day long.'" And he recognized and appreciated that playing against the best drew out his best. "I'd love to play against Irvin every game.

"Irvin will talk back to you, too," he added delightedly. In mock disgust, he offered the contrast presented by Auburn star Lawyer Tillman. "He was very quiet. He made me mad. He wouldn't talk back."

Sometimes, an opponent simply had no rebuttal. Deion read during a flight to play Michigan State in 1987 that Spartans star Andre Rison had described him as just another defensive back. Sanders throttled him. Rison had one reception, late in the game, for 6 yards. At one point, Sanders said, he told Rison, "I saw you on film and you looked great. The film must have lied."

Many were the receivers warned early in the game that when it was over, they'd be losing their scholarships. Sanders actually forfeited his scholarship but not his eligibility when George Steinbrenner signed him to a minor-league baseball contract worth a reported $60,000 for six weeks split among Sarasota (rookie league), Fort Lauderdale (Class A), and Columbus, Ohio (Class AAA), the summer of 1988.

That would become the equivalent of pocket change once Deion and his gold $ medallion departed Tallahassee for pro riches.

# T-Buck: Never a Dull Moment

Terrell Buckley dared to be great. He knew no fear. A short memory is imperative for any cornerback, whose mistakes happen so glaringly in open field. You'd swear watching Buckley that he'd developed amnesia from one poor play until the next snap.

He gambled often. Sometimes he got burned. But he didn't stop gambling. "Buckley's a momentum guy for somebody," Bowden once quipped after a trademark performance in which Buckley atoned for one gaffe with several marvelous plays. "When he makes a move, somebody's fixin' to gain momentum." To Buckley, the reward was worth the risk.

It takes a healthy dose of audacity to put yourself in position to intercept 30 passes in high school (in Pascagoula, Mississippi) and 21 more in a three-year college career. Buckley swiped twelve in the record-setting junior season that made him Florida State's second Thorpe Award winner and prompted him to turn pro a year early.

Nobody was more eager to see him go than Will Furrer, a competent quarterback at Virginia Tech who saw Buckley's entry into the 1992 NFL draft (the Green Bay Packers selected him fifth) as long overdue. Buckley intercepted a Furrer pass and returned it 53 yards for a crucial touchdown in FSU's 39–28 victory over the Hokies in 1990. A year later he victimized Furrer for a pair of interceptions and a 71-yard touchdown return in a 33–20 FSU escape. "When is someone going to draft Terrell Buckley and get him in the pros where he belongs?" an exasperated Furrer asked.

Bobby Bowden concluded after the 1990 game, "Terrell Buckley made the play of the game." He paused, weighed what he had just said, then added as if talking to himself, "I wonder how many times he has made the play of the game. That may be the fourth straight game."

Like Sanders before him, Buckley relished nothing more than that instant transition from defense to offense. "When I pick one off," he said, "I feel I have a 95 percent chance of returning it [for a touchdown]. Those are linemen out there [trying to track him down]."

True, 95 percent defies reality. But Buckley returned 4 interceptions for touchdowns during his career, matching the record set by Sanders. And he hauled back 3 punts for scores, again sharing that FSU mark with Deion and mid-1980s special-teams demon Joe Wessel. Also like Sanders, Buckley derived his greatest satisfaction and joy from matching skills with a receiver of comparable acclaim. Of one heralded rival he said, "I wouldn't mind playing against him every week, simply because that's competition and that's what I live for." Does that sentiment sound familiar?

Buckley was speaking about Desmond Howard, the Michigan marvel who collected the Heisman Trophy at the end of the 1991 season with a landslide-voting margin over FSU quarterback Casey Weldon.

Terrell Buckley, a risk taker who frequently was rewarded with interceptions, swiped an FSU-record 21 during his flashy career.

Buckley established the tone for the Seminoles' exhilarating 51–31 victory at jam-packed Michigan Stadium by baiting Wolverines quarterback Elvis Grbac into a quick sideline pass toward Howard on the game's second offensive snap. He broke forward, intercepted, and romped 40 yards untouched for the first touchdown of a matchup of teams ranked number one and number three nationally.

"A team like that is going to try to get their big-play man into the offense quick," he said later. "I read the three-step drop. [Howard's route] was either going to be an 'out' or a slant, and he was lined up too close for the slant." Grbac threw 12 passes toward Howard that brilliant afternoon. Howard caught 4 (for 69 yards); Buckley intercepted 2.

Howard produced 2 of Michigan's 4 touchdowns. On the second, Buckley had him so tightly tended that when Buckley tried to raise his right arm to deflect Grbac's pass at the goal line, it got caught under Howard's left arm and shortened his leap.

Asked afterwards how he'd assess the matchup of All-Americans, Buckley flashed an infectious grin and said, "Tie ballgame!" Two superb players; 2 touchdowns to 2 interceptions. But the scoreboard was the tiebreaker.

## Abraham: FSU's "Avis" CB

Clifton Abraham, raised in the infamous Oak Cliff section of South Dallas, did not flaunt the talent of a Deion Sanders or a Terrell Buckley or possibly up to a half-dozen other cornerbacks in the position's rich history at FSU. But it's doubtful anybody ever squeezed more out of the talent he was given. A reporter isn't supposed to play favorites, particularly in any way that distorts reality. But cover a program for twenty consecutive years and witness the development and maturation of so many players through their entire careers, and it's impossible not to develop a rooting interest in certain individuals.

A photograph in the *Miami Herald* the morning after FSU achieved its first national championship with its Orange Bowl victory over Nebraska remains a vivid snapshot on his career. Abraham, having already hurled his helmet into the air, is

Clifton Abraham, 1994 All-America cornerback.

in midleap with joy contorting his facial features. The picture epitomized that "one shining moment" NCAA basketball theme.

But the lasting memory I have of Abraham has little to do with his three seasons as a starter for the Seminoles, his two all-Atlantic Coast Conference awards, or the 1994 All-America recognition. It has everything to do with what made him tick and the mean streets he had survived.

An interview we did the summer before that 1994 season ranks with the most poignant I've ever conducted because Abraham was so open about his adventures growing up. And we're not talking about a fistfight in the school yard. Abraham told about a street party he attended with a bunch of his Carter High School and neighborhood buddies, including a friend named Quincy Green. He remembered dropping his hat and bending over to pick it up, no more than an arm's length from Green.

"That's when I heard, 'Pow! Pow! Pow! Pow!'" he said. Bullets were flying from a passing car. "Everybody's first instinct is to run," he said. The partiers scattered. But Green fell, "like he was tired," Abraham said. "We started laughing. We were like, 'Man, I thought you were in shape.'"

But when they spotted blood gathering around neck and chest wounds, the laughter died. So did Quincy Green.

"Oak Cliff's a very tough area," Abraham explained that day. "A lot of crime. Everybody's into drugs and sex and everything else." That's why he so desperately wanted to get his mother and younger brother and sister out of the area. "My momma knows I have a plan, a focus. She knows I'm her last hope."

Time was critical. It already was too late for Abraham's twin brothers. One had served time in prison for aggravated battery in a robbery of a fast-food business. The other was in a maximum-security prison in Huntsville, Texas, for aggravated assault on a police officer resulting from an auto theft.

Clifton admitted that he might have swirled in the same cesspool. Only because a girl friend had complained that he wasn't spending enough time with her did Abraham reject an invitation to hang out with a bunch of teammates one night in May 1989. His friends robbed an area store and got caught. Fifteen people in a loose robbery ring were arrested. Five of them were Carter

High teammates of Abraham's. They went to prison. Had he decided to hang out with his buddies that night, he said, "I definitely wouldn't have been here, know what I'm saying?" They were teenagers. Peer pressure would have made it too easy to go along.

But you couldn't know Abraham without acknowledging that more than coincidence kept him from teetering onto the wrong side of the law. He was a hair shy of 5'9" tall. But he would not accept size as a deterrent. "People who might think I'm too small don't know what's inside of me," he said.

He expected no favors. He knew he'd have to work for everything. "Every stat I've got at the end of a season, I made it happen," he said. "I haven't lucked into anything. I don't get tipped balls, underthrown balls, overthrown balls . . . I've never had any lollipops in my stats."

Abraham never had any "lollipops" in his life. But that didn't stand in his way. Mickey Andrews appreciated Abraham's inner drive. "I don't think I've had to say one word to Clif, ever, about his effort . . . Football is a way to help him get what he wants—a better life, a better environment—than what he was raised in."

Despite his size limitations, Abraham managed to play for all or parts of six seasons in the NFL and Canadian Football League. He's the personification of a cliché but a truism nonetheless—that you can't measure heart.

# Finally, a Championship

The Orange Bowl showdown for the 1993 national championship had more trapdoors for prohibitive favorite Florida State than a carnival fun house. This had shaped up as a setup from the outset, an invitation for the Seminoles to swallow the hype after a premature toast to the coronation. Now, with exultant FSU fans and relieved players erupting in celebration of college football's ultimate prize, one so wrenchingly denied the Seminoles so often, officials were returning 1 second to Miami Stadium's scoreboard clock.

Players already had dumped a bucket of ice and ade over the head of their sixty-four-year-old coach, hitting him with the container and practically knocking him to his knees in the process. Now Bobby Bowden was being informed that Nebraska, undefeated but a 17-point underdog in oddsmakers' eyes, would have that single second to reverse history and deliver heartbreak.

Ann Bowden, the wife of FSU's coach, stopped in midcelebration with her children and grandchildren in the stands and, in an emotional U-turn, anticipated the worst. "I just didn't think it was meant to be," she later told the *Miami Herald*'s Dan Le Batard outside the stadium. "Moses wasn't allowed to go to the promised land. Coach Bowden wasn't allowed to win the national championship."

Nebraska's field-goal unit trotted onto the field as the drenched and stunned Bowden and his players returned to their sideline. The lead already had been swapped twice in the previous 75 seconds of high drama. Byron Bennett had staked the Cornhuskers to a 16–15 advantage with a 27-yard field goal with 1:16 remaining. Freshman Scott Bentley had returned FSU to apparent 18–16 command with a 22-yard field goal but left 21 seconds after a classic case of clock mismanagement.

The last of those 21 seconds ticked off the scoreboard as FSU defenders bulldogged tight end Trumane Bell at the FSU 28 yard line after a 29-yard pass from Huskers quarterback Tommie Frazier. Game over? No, said the officials. The clock should have been stopped at 0:01. Now Bennett lined up for a 45-yard field goal and a 19–18 Nebraska victory that would rank with football's most monumental upsets.

The kick left his foot . . . and never had a chance. Bennett yanked it so far to the left that it was clear immediately he had misfired. Ann Bowden's darkest fears were not realized. It was meant for her husband to win that championship so tantalizingly within reach but so elusive in every season since 1987.

Afterwards Bowden put the football fates in perspective. "We've lost national championships, we feel, by missing kicks," he said. "Today we finally won one when somebody else missed a kick."

Yes, final ballots in contentious Associated Press and CNN/USA *Today* polls remained to be cast. And the prebowl debate that had raged over who truly deserved to play for the national title would be sustained after the bowls by a vocal minority who believed once-beaten Notre Dame should receive the ultimate reward for dealing FSU its lone loss.

Before the bowls, West Virginia Coach Don Nehlen had lobbied passionately for those with votes to support a battle of unbeatens, his 11–0 Mountaineers against 11–0 Nebraska. In his view, FSU's 31–24 stumble at Notre Dame in a November classic matching number one– and number two–ranked teams disqualified the Seminoles.

But anyone who factored schedule difficulty into the equation could not buy that reasoning. And Nehlen's excusable campaign looked hollow after the same Florida team that FSU subdued, 33–21, in the regular-season finale at Gainesville drubbed West Virginia, 41–7, in the Sugar Bowl.

An unbeaten Auburn team that reeled off eleven consecutive victories under a first-year head coach could have splashed fuel on the flames. But the Tigers were on probation and banned from a postseason bowl. Besides, that first-year coach would have had to avoid family reunions if he had spoken out in any fashion damaging FSU prospects. Terry Bowden chose instead to extol the might of his father's Seminoles.

The prebowl polls shook out this way:

**Associated Press (media members)**
1. Florida State
2. Nebraska
3. West Virginia

**CNN/USA *Today* (coaches)**
1. Nebraska
2. West Virginia
3. Florida State

But the second-year Bowl Coalition dictated a title match involving the two teams with most points combined from the two polls. The Bowl Coalition result, with final points:

1. Nebraska (2,987)
2. Florida State (2,953)
3. West Virginia (2,889)

Coach Lou Holtz and Notre Dame chafed over a muted role in the debate. One week after knocking the Seminoles from the number one perch in both polls, the Irish—on home turf again—fell to number seventeen Boston College, 41–39, on David Gordon's last-second 41-yard field goal. They would resurface, understandably but not emphatically. Notre Dame, like Florida State, was severely tested in its bowl. A field goal with

2:22 left salvaged a 24–21 Cotton Bowl victory over Texas A&M.

Bowden knew that if FSU and West Virginia won their bowls, the voting coaches would sustain their support of the Mountaineers and produce a split national championship. To him, a share of a championship would have been palatable. He also recognized that FSU and Notre Dame bowl victories with a West Virginia loss could revive sentiment for the Irish.

But between Bennett's last-gasp field-goal attempt and announcement of the final vote, Bowden assessed FSU's right to the CNN/USA *Today* title this way: "I was thinking, 'We were number three, Notre Dame was number four, and we beat number one. How are they going to throw Notre Dame up ahead of us? They got a [bowl] scare just like we did.'"

He woke up to a unified title. FSU received forty-six first-place votes to Notre Dame's twelve in the Associated Press poll and thirty-six first-place votes to Notre Dame's twenty-five in the CNN/USA *Today* balloting.

Holtz's disappointment was understandable. Ordinarily, any debate over two once-beaten teams that previously had played each other would automatically favor the head-to-head winner. But FSU wide receiver Tamarick Vanover probably captured the majority viewpoint when he reasoned, "Notre Dame lost to a lower-ranked team [Boston College] at home, where we had to [travel] to play the number two team, and they had two weeks to prepare for us."

Just as a jury is commanded to weigh the entire body of evidence, poll voters must assess performance over an entire season. A review reveals just how potent this FSU team had been. Nebraska free safety John Reece expressed conventional wisdom

# Number 77 from Mariel

Idalia Sanabria's eight-year-old son sat wide-eyed and silent with his mother as the storm tossed the shrimp boat from wave to wave on its perilous 1980 journey from Mariel, Cuba, to south Florida. The *Venetia II* had a capacity of about two hundred, she estimated, but probably double that number crowded its decks.

Sanabria had been assigned to a smaller boat that departed two hours before the *Venetia II*. But a family of four behind them in line included a wheelchair-confined child who was ill. The family begged Sanabria for her two places on the boat so they could travel together. "My mom gave up our spot for them," the boy recalled years later.

The merciful act saved the lives of Sanabria and her son. "Because our boat was bigger," she related through an interpreter, "we caught up to where we could see the little boat ahead of us. We saw it capsize and go into like a whirlpool. We saw them all die . . . We saw the sea swallow them."

Sanabria was reliving that horrifying memory in a tiny café called La Gata on Northwest 36th Street in Miami. She had purchased it for $6,000, and she made the place vibrate with life.

On the wall opposite the serving area and behind the thirteen counter stools, she had assembled a virtual shrine to the son who had survived the boat lift with her. There were plaques and pennants and pictures. Lots of pictures. Number 77 with Bobby Bowden. Number 77 in a blocking convoy for tailback Sean Jackson. Number 77 with Renegade the Appaloosa.

His early years adapting to a new country and a new language had been an uphill struggle for Sanabria's son, Jesus Hernandez. But the will to persist and prevail served him well when he walked on at Florida State and, in his second year, earned a football scholarship.

He shared playing time at one tackle spot with Juan Laureano as a third-year sophomore on the 1993 national championship team. He earned All-Atlantic Coast Conference honors as a senior in 1995. He did that against all odds for a walk-on. But consider the odds he overcame just getting to U.S. shores.

when he said during the buildup to the Orange Bowl, "Before that Notre Dame game, we had an image that there's no way these guys could be beaten." It sure looked that way for a long while. Here's a game-by-game synopsis.

## Kickoff Classic: FSU 42, Kansas 0

Charlie Ward engineered a workmanlike 538-yard attack enhancing a preseason view that the Heisman Trophy was his to lose. But the opener focused on a defense that was the supposed Achilles' heel of this contender.

FSU led, 14-0, in the second quarter when Kansas failed on seven plays from the FSU 1 yard line to cross the goal. In all, because of a pass-interference penalty and three offside infractions against the Seminoles, the Jayhawks snapped the ball twelve times inside the 10-yard line on that one possession but failed to score.

Defensive coordinator Mickey Andrews—not easily pleased— marveled, "I've not seen anything like that as long as I've been involved in football, playing, and coaching."

## FSU 45, Duke 7

Lightning bolts on a wet, stormy night delayed the start at Duke for fifteen minutes, but for the Blue Devils, that proved only a stay of execution. The Seminoles did take a while to get their footing on a mushy playing surface. They led only 7–0 into the second quarter but reeled off 22 points in the next ten minutes.

*Charlie Ward (17), here accompanied by center Clay Shiver (53), gave defensive coordinators headaches with his open-field scampers.*

"Those were the worst field conditions I've ever played in," Ward said. But FSU still netted 628 yards, 231 of those on Ward's 22-for-31 passing accuracy with a wet ball before he retired in the third quarter. Duke's only points came on a 1-yard "drive" after a blocked punt.

Oh, and FSU linebacker Derrick Brooks sprinted 32 yards to score after intercepting a pass. That was a mere footnote then, but it became more in subsequent weeks.

# FSU 57, Clemson 0

This rout needed comic relief, and freshman quarterback Danny Kanell, fullback William Floyd, and FSU's bizarre "Kentucky Derby" unit provided it. Why coaches did it remains a mystery, but on the first play after an early-game change of possession, they'd routinely hustle the second offensive unit onto the field to run one quick play and then get back to the bench.

Ordinarily the call was for a quick pitch and a sweep. This time they were going to allow Kanell to pass. Even as they ran onto the field, excited receivers were urging Kanell not to throw an interception or that would be the last time coaches risked a pass with the Kentucky Derby reserves. Kanell, intent on looking over the defense, lined up not behind center but behind his right guard. Floyd looked up, stricken, and joked later, "I'm thinking, 'Oh, man, I'm about to play quarterback'" with a snap past the misplaced Kanell.

Floyd urgently stepped forward and practically lifted Kanell over behind center. Kanell took the snap and teamed with tight end Lonnie Johnson on a 78-yard touchdown play.

Ho-hum! Charlie Ward completed 25 of 33 passes for 317 yards and 4 touchdowns. Oh, and Derrick Brooks scooped up a Clemson fumble and sprinted 83 yards for a touchdown and blocked a punt that cornerback Clifton Abraham retrieved for another 6 points.

"After today's game," Bowden cracked, "I'm confining my coaching to just Brooks and Ward."

# FSU 33, North Carolina 7

Commissioner Gene Corrigan reportedly threatened to resign in the fall of 1990 when a trio of schools appeared ready to block an invitation to Florida State to join the Atlantic Coast Conference. He successfully lobbied for the 6–2 vote needed for approval. The night of September 18, 1993, in Chapel Hill, North Carolina, lived up to Corrigan's vision and proved his wisdom. The focus on football in a perceived basketball conference justified the firm stance he had taken two years earlier.

Not only were Mack Brown's Tar Heels ranked number thirteen, but North Carolina was playing host to a number one–ranked opponent for the first time since a 1953 visit by Notre Dame. The atmosphere was electric, and a national television audience (ESPN) would witness the game.

FSU battled to a shaky 10–7 halftime lead before sealing a victory with a 17-point third quarter fueled by Derrick Brooks's third touchdown in four games. He intercepted a pass and returned it 49 yards. Said Bobby Bowden, "I can never remember a defensive player making so many big plays as Derrick Brooks has made this year. Even Deion Sanders." At FSU, mentioning anyone in the same breath with Sanders, a two-time consensus All-American, automatically elevated that player to icon stature.

# FSU 51, Georgia Tech 0

A year after a 29–24 victory at Georgia Tech gave birth to FSU's "fast break" attack and served as a coming-out party for Charlie

Ward, a rout of the Yellow Jackets that featured Ward's 21-for-28 passing represented a necessary nuisance. Miami week finally was upon the Seminoles.

"All these wins we've got?" Bobby Bowden questioned rhetorically after number one FSU continued to bulldoze rivals. "They don't mean a thing if we don't win next week. Next week we find out." The Hurricanes would invade with a number three ranking and seven victories in the previous eight meetings between the rivals.

But FSU looked primed. Ward and Company amassed 582 yards to Georgia Tech's 110 in the Seminole defense's third shutout in five games. Nobody was ready to dispute William Floyd's matter-of-fact observation, "It's going to take a lot of things going against us for us not to win the national championship." Through five games, FSU had scored 228 points and allowed 14. Derrick Brooks alone had outscored Kansas, Duke, Clemson, North Carolina, and Georgia Tech 3 touchdowns to 2.

Here's a note for later reference on voters' ultimate support of FSU. The Associated Press poll at this juncture was as follows:

1. FSU
2. Alabama
3. Miami
4. Notre Dame
5. Florida

The second half of FSU's season featured the home game against Miami and trips to Notre Dame and Florida.

And here's how impressed Las Vegas oddsmakers had become with the Seminoles: They made FSU a 12½-point favorite over the number three–ranked team in the nation.

# FSU 28, Miami 10

Freshman Scott Bentley, who was recruited to erase the agony of FSU's "Wide Right I" and "Wide Right II" losses to the Hurricanes the previous two seasons, discovered quickly what a critical role he had assumed on the national scene. *Sports Illustrated* made the Aurora, Colorado, kicker its preseason cover boy before he'd ever attended a college class.

Here's the history: Gerry Thomas attempted a 34-yard field goal to erase a 17–16 Miami lead in the final seconds of the 1991 meeting. He missed, wide right. A year later Dan Mowrey attempted a 39-yard field goal in the closing seconds on Miami's Orange Bowl turf to forge a 19–19 tie. He missed, wide right.

Bobby Bowden properly assessed the weight on Bentley in the days leading up to the showdown with the Hurricanes. "There's no way [Bentley] could practice for that kind of pressure," he said. "If he weren't going through this, Dan Mowrey would be going through the same thing . . . Somebody's got to face that pressure, and the guy who has to face it is whoever the kicker is at Florida State."

But Charlie Ward said, "We didn't want it to come down to a field goal." And his 256 passing yards and the combined 165 rushing yards by tailbacks Sean Jackson and Warrick Dunn provided the impetus for the 21–10 advantage nursed into the final seven minutes. Still, there was concern.

Devin Bush, Miami native and FSU safety, squelched it. With about five minutes remaining, he darted in front of a Frank Costa pass, intercepted, and sprinted 40 yards to a clinching touchdown that ended Miami's thirty-one-game regular-season winning streak.

"My eyes got this big," a delighted Bush said of Costa's telegraphed pass. "I had deep coverage on the other side, and I could see there wasn't a deep threat on my side. I didn't figure they'd run the tight end deep, so I cheated over."

## FSU 40, Virginia 14

The Cavaliers arrived with a perfect 5–0 record and a number fifteen ranking. But Bobby Bowden worried about a psychological letdown nonetheless. "Usually after Miami, we take [the frustration of a loss] out on the next team," he said. "But we beat Miami. We may not know how to act."

Ward, the personification of "even keel," knew how to act. His 86-yard touchdown hookup with Tamarick Vanover launched a sequence of seven possessions that produced 5 touchdowns and a field goal. He reportedly had been suffering from slight tendonitis in his elbow. It didn't show as he completed 23 of 31 passes for 322 yards and 3 scores.

FSU's defense suffered a couple of uncharacteristic breakdowns, and linebacker Ken Alexander, an academic All-American, expressed the perspective that reflected defensive coordinator Mickey Andrews's demands for excellence. "It's like taking a test," Alexander said. "You're disappointed when you know you're supposed to make an A and you make a B-plus."

# FSU 54, Wake Forest 0

Overriding any joy from the defense's fourth shutout in eight games and a 647-yard attack on a gray, rainy day was the dark cloud suddenly hovering over Charlie Ward. He suffered bruised ribs in the area of his sternum and left shoulder when gang-tackled late in the first half of a rout. The implications were obvious as doctors tended to him.

"You could almost feel the crowd cringe," center Clay Shiver said.

Ward wasn't missed in the second half because freshman Warrick Dunn was emerging as a bona fide threat. He pranced 63 yards for a touchdown, escaped 58 yards on another run, and finished with 162 yards in 8 carries for a 20.25-yard average. But Notre Dame was only two weeks off, with a trip to Maryland in the interim.

# FSU 49, Maryland 20

Dr. Dan Kanell, the Dolphins team physician, adjusted his travel plans so that he could attend the Seminoles game at College Park, Maryland, on Saturday on the way to a Dolphins-Jets game in East Rutherford, New Jersey, on Sunday. His detour proved worthwhile.

Danny Kanell Jr., alerted by coach Mark Richt after the pregame breakfast that he would start against the Terrapins, became the first FSU quarterback to pass for 5 touchdowns in a

*A common sight at FSU games in the mid-1990s was Warrick Dunn in flight and defenders in hopeless pursuit.*

game since Peter Tom Willis in the 41–17 Fiesta Bowl rout of Nebraska that capped FSU's 1989 season.

Kanell's mother, Diane, would have shouted herself hoarse but already had laryngitis. "I'm glad it's over," she rasped happily afterwards. "I just feel so weak. I was really nervous." That's OK. Her son wasn't. He completed 28 of 38 passes for 341 yards without interception.

Richt said afterwards, "We could have played [Ward], and then, if he got hit in the chest [and couldn't play at Notre Dame], everybody would have called us idiots."

Bobby Bowden, aware of the upcoming test within sight of the Golden Dome and Touchdown Jesus, said, "Charlie will go . . . unless a train runs over him."

## Notre Dame 31, FSU 24

A Notre Dame locomotive, in the form of Lee Becton, Ray Zellars, and Jeff Burris convoyed by a massive wall of blockers, steamrolled Florida State's defense as the number two Fighting Irish all but derailed the number one–ranked Seminoles' national-championship express.

The conventional wisdom in coaching was that if you were playing a Lou Holtz team and he had two weeks to prepare, beware. That proved out as the Irish summoned all that leprechaun magic to supplement Holtz's motivational and strategic expertise.

Burris, NFL–bound as a safety, was Holtz's secret weapon. He was shifted into a full-house backfield and scored a pair of touchdowns in the midst of a 239-yard power ground game that featured 26 punishing Becton carries for 122 yards. Part of a marvelously executed game plan was to control the clock and minimize Charlie Ward's opportunities.

Ward, showing rust from his time off and troubled early by brisk, swirling winds, had to engineer a swift scoring strike midway through the fourth quarter just to carve into a 31–17 deficit.

But he was firing into the end zone for a potential tie in the final seconds. Safety Shawn Wooden swatted down Ward's last-gasp pass aimed at Warrick Dunn.

Typical of him, Ward kept perspective afterwards. "Some guys were open," he said of the final, futile bid to salvage victory. "I can't rethink my decision . . . [but] if I could run the play again, I had Matt Frier wide open." He had passed for 297 yards and 3 touchdowns, but it had not been a vintage performance.

Wide receiver Kevin Knox squelched talk of Notre Dame's rich history in the aftermath. "When they snapped the ball, I don't know about you but I didn't see any ghosts flying around out there," he said. "Mystique? Mystique is a myth."

But Bobby Bowden amended that. "No doubt about the great spirit they have," he said. "The mystique didn't hurt us. But it helps them. Those kids were just possessed."

## FSU 62, North Carolina State 3

In the locker room at Notre Dame, players had barely taken a deep breath before a couple of Seminoles began lobbying for an FSU–Notre Dame rematch in a bowl. "No doubt," wide receiver Matt Frier responded when asked whether one would be warranted. "You just saw one of the best football games of all time in one of the great stadiums of all time . . . If we sputter against N.C. State on Saturday or Florida in The Swamp, give [the chance] to somebody else. But if you want to see the two best teams in the country, get these two together again."

But one Saturday later, while Charlie Ward was reasserting

himself as a surefire Heisman Trophy winner with 4 touchdown passes and 1 touchdown run to dispose of the Wolfpack, Notre Dame stumbled.

The Irish, puffed up by the upset of FSU, found themselves in an uphill fight from a 38–17 deficit in the fourth quarter. They mounted a desperate rally to a 39–38 lead on Kevin McDougal's 4-yard touchdown pass to Lake Dawson with 1:09 remaining. But Boston College quarterback Glenn Foley directed an answering drive from his own 10 yard line to a winning 41-yard field goal by David Gordon on the final snap. The kick went into the same north end zone into which Ward had been firing on the final snap a week earlier.

Notre Dame's regular season was over. FSU's wasn't. The final test would be at Florida Field, where the Gators had not lost in Steve Spurrier's four seasons pulling the coaching strings.

"Going into the season," Bobby Bowden warned, "we knew there would be three mountain peaks [to scale], and playing Florida at Florida will be every bit as tough as playing Notre Dame at Notre Dame."

## FSU 33, Florida 21

A seemingly insurmountable 27–7 lead built on Charlie Ward's 3 touchdown passes had dwindled to 27–21, and the din at Florida Field threatened to burst eardrums within a 25-mile radius when a pair of quiet FSU stars delivered a thunderclap that silenced Gators revelers.

Terry Dean had replaced freshman quarterback Danny Wuerffel at halftime and proceeded to solve one third-down or fourth-down problem after another in a clutch passing performance reminiscent of John Elway. Suddenly, with about six minutes left, FSU was reeling.

Momentum was such that if Florida got the ball right back, a touchdown and go-ahead extra point seemed a given to panicky Seminole fans. Ward's first-down and second-down passes were batted back at him by Gators Kevin Carter and William Gaines. A deafening roar grew by decibels. On third down, again blocking broke down and Ward scrambled to his left as Florida tackle Ellis Johnson grasped for him.

That's when roommates Ward and Dunn, both of whom preferred to let actions speak for them, saved a game and a season and left Florida fans dumbstruck. "I was just running an 'out' route," Dunn said in a raucous locker room minutes later. "I saw Charlie was scrambling, and I just went into our scrambling drill. I turned it up the sideline."

Ward's pass led him perfectly, and Dunn, at full stride, whisked past linebacker Ed Robinson and didn't slow until he'd crossed the goal line 79 yards from where the play had started.

"That's what it takes to win big games," Bowden capsulized. "Big-time players making big plays." FSU was bound for the Orange Bowl and one victory from the one trophy that had eluded them.

# Husker House of Horrors

The Orange Bowl showdown the night of January 1, 1994, ensured that either Florida State's Bobby Bowden or Nebraska counterpart Tom Osborne would fill a glaring void in otherwise admirable résumés. Both were among college football's most successful coaches, and neither had celebrated a national championship.

Odds favored Bowden. His FSU teams had won eight consecutive bowl games. Nebraska had been defeated in six straight bowls under Osborne. Asked to explain the Cornhuskers' postseason failures, Osborne quipped, "Probably because I keep running into Bobby."

The Seminoles and Cornhuskers had finished the season against each other three times in the previous six years. FSU won the 1988 Fiesta Bowl, 31–28; the 1990 Fiesta Bowl, 41–17; and the 1993 Orange Bowl, 27–14.

What Osborne did not say is that when Nebraska didn't have to square off against FSU, he frequently found himself preparing a bowl invitee to play the University of Miami on its Orange Bowl home turf.

To that point, the 1983 Nebraska team was Osborne's best. That star-studded team had ripped through a 12–0 regular season at a 52-points-per-game clip with an average margin of victory of 36.5. But its "reward" was a road trip. Awaiting them in the Orange Bowl were Howard Schnellenberger's number five–ranked Hurricanes and quarterback Bernie Kosar, who had reeled off ten consecutive victories after an opening 28–3 loss at Florida.

Nebraska got blindsided. Kosar's 2 touchdown passes fueled a 17-point first quarter. After the Cornhuskers had battled back into a tie in the third quarter, the Hurricanes rebuilt their lead to 31–17 with sustained drives to 2 touchdowns five minutes apart.

Again Osborne's team rallied, and reserve I-back Jeff Smith escaped 24 yards to pare the UM advantage to 31–30 with 48 seconds remaining. A point-after kick would forge a 31–31 tie and an all-but-certain Nebraska national championship. Osborne opted for a two-point conversion attempt. He said simply that Nebraska had come to win and to complete a perfect season. Quarterback Turner Gill's pass deflected off UM safety Ken Calhoun's fingertips, hit Smith in a shoulder pad, and fell harmlessly to the ground. Winner: UM. National champion: UM.

Ten years later, again in the Orange Bowl, Nebraska failed on a two-point conversion attempt into that same end zone. After Lawrence Phillips dashed 12 yards for a touchdown on the first snap of the fourth quarter, quarterback Tommie Frazier's bid for a 15–15 tie fell a yard short when he was knocked out of bounds keeping on an option play.

The Huskers again looked like they'd finally reward Osborne with a national championship when Byron Bennett kicked his 27-yard field goal with 1:16 remaining. But fullback William Floyd's 2-yard plunge on fourth-down-and-one near midfield sustained a drive to Scott Bentley's winning 22-yard kick. A swing pass from Charlie Ward to tailback Warrick Dunn ate up 23 yards in the winning drive, with a 15-yard bonus for a late-hit penalty on Nebraska cornerback Barron Miles. A makeable field goal became a chip shot for Bentley after a pass-interference penalty.

Osborne, however, got a championship ring twelve months later, again in the Orange Bowl, this time against Miami. The Huskers wore down the Hurricanes and rallied to a 24–17 victory. A year later, Osborne's Huskers buried Steve Spurrier's Florida team, 62–24, in the Fiesta Bowl. After the crushing loss to Florida State, Nebraska did not lose again until two games into the 1996 season.

# "But He Played Miami"

The coach's postmortems for members of the media the morning after home games are delivered at a Tallahassee hotel. Delighted or deflated, Bobby Bowden shows up. On this November 1991 Sunday morning, before a gathering expanded by more national reporters than usual, Bowden was uncharacteristically depressed. He clearly had lost sleep reliving the most tormenting plays from the 17–16 loss to the University of Miami that derailed a 10–0 FSU team.

The setback, which gave birth to the burdensome "wide right" hex that would continue to bedevil the Seminoles into the twenty-first century, took its toll on Bowden. "When I die," he said reflectively, "they'll chisel on my tombstone, 'But he played Miami.'"

Not only was the loss the ninth in twelve typically brutal FSU-Miami slugfests dating back to 1980, it was the fourth in that span by a single point. Salting the wounds and prolonging the pain, three of the four UM teams that survived those gut-wrenchers reigned as national champs.

"One lousy point and I've got to say they're better than us," Bowden grumbled.

If that's not torturous enough, Miami isn't even Florida State's most bitter rival. That distinction is accorded Florida. Blood boils in that one. There's a rancor not evident in the Miami series despite how often a national title has been on the line between Seminoles and Hurricanes.

Bowden admitted cheerily after FSU subdued Florida, 23–12, in 1998, "Beating Florida is more important [to his fans and boosters] than winning a national championship, I think. I think our people feel that way. Whatever makes them happy makes Bobby happy."

Though the Seminoles count two national championship seasons among the fourteen in succession that produced ten or more victories and no worse than a final number five ranking in major polls, the Hurricanes or Gators conceivably deprived Bowden's program of as many as seven other national titles. How weighty is *that* nugget?

"My junior and senior years we were 22–2," defensive tackle Steve Gabbard observed of an FSU career climaxed by the 1988 season. "Both losses were to Miami. They cost us two rings."

The 1991 FSU team quarterbacked by Casey Weldon plunged into such a funk over the 17–16 loss to Miami—which came down to Gerry Thomas's errant 34-yard field goal—that even a game at Florida two weeks later failed to regenerate signs of life. FSU staggered to a 14–9 loss.

This is subject to debate, naturally, but I'm convinced that had Thomas's right foot delivered a 19–17 victory, those Seminoles would have emerged from Gainesville 12–0 and finished 13–0 with a championship trophy no matter who lined up against them in a bowl. "Losing that Miami game . . . we were done," Weldon recalled later. "It was all over. It shouldn't have been, but . . . " He shrugged. "I never realized until those last two games how much pressure had built." A 44–28 rout of Ty Detmer and Brigham Young launched a season highlighted by road victories over Michigan and Louisiana State that kept increasing the stakes.

Remember that through this FSU era of excellence, no Bowden team managed an unblemished record until 1999. Over the years this provoked the asinine "can't-win-the-big-one" comment, a critique that rankles me no matter the pro franchise or college program besmirched. You don't play in the "big one" unless you already have won one or more big ones. (Or, as Bowden once concluded, "I've finally figured out what the 'big one' is. It's the one you lose.")

"People ask me, 'How come you always end up with a loss?'" he related on another occasion. "I tell them we're the only team that plays Miami and Florida every year." He didn't bother to add that FSU must play one or the other on the road every season. It's no coincidence that both of his national championship teams survived severe tests in a regular-season finale at Florida.

In the fourteen seasons from 1987 through 2000, Florida State absorbed the mind-numbing total of only nineteen losses with one tie. Eleven of the losses and the tie came in games against the two in-state rivals. Of the seven one-loss seasons, Miami or Florida administered that loss six times.

For the trivia-minded, here are the other eight losses: Brett Favre–quarterbacked Southern Mississippi and Clemson in 1989, Auburn in 1990, Notre Dame in 1993, Virginia in 1995, North Carolina State and Tennessee (national championship game) in 1998, and Oklahoma (national championship game) in 2000.

Miami and Florida would be comparably damaged if they crossed swords annually on a home-and-away basis. But Florida aborted their annual series after the 1987 season, and the Hurricanes and Gators have played each other rarely since.

Even before all three programs had achieved elite status regularly, Bowden said in 1985, "They can talk about the Big Eight and the Big Ten and the Southeastern Conference, but the Big Florida ain't bad."

In each of eighteen seasons starting with Miami's 1983 national championship, at least one of the state's three powers finished with a top-five Associated Press ranking, and in twelve of those eighteen seasons, two of the trio have been counted among the top five. Remarkably Miami and FSU finished 1–2 in 1987, 2–3 in 1988, and 1–3 in 1989. Similarly Florida and FSU ranked 2–4 in 1995, 1–3 in 1996, 4–3 in 1997, and 5–3 in 1998.

Again using the parameters of 1987 and 2000, Florida State posted a 7–7 record against Miami, 11–4–1 against Florida, and 134–8 against the rest of the college football world. For the record, during that fourteen-season span, Miami accounted for three national championships and Florida for one. Total for the "Big Florida"—six.

## Curse of the 'Canes

Starting in 1987, heartbreak has become habit for Florida State against nemesis Miami. Rarely had a team been so dominating for three quarters and so devastated in the fourth as the Seminoles in a monumental 26–25 loss in October that determined which team ranked number one and which ranked number two once all the chips had been played three months later. It was the lone loss for either team that year.

A 19–3 FSU lead late in the third quarter probably should have been more like 35–3, except for a handful of bizarre special-teams plays highlighted by an early 51-yard swap of field position when a premature snap sailed past unsuspecting holder Danny McManus and kicker Derek Schmidt. *Miami Herald* columnist Edwin Pope wrote that it was "the zaniest game in Miami's history." The word *surreal* appeared appropriately in game accounts.

With 2:35 remaining in that third quarter, Miami's offense had netted a total of 90 yards on 30 snaps. The Hurricanes had failed to gain a first down on five of their seven series. On the flip side, FSU tailback Sammie Smith was hammering toward a 189-

# A 31–31 Victory

Danny Kanell Jr.'s niche in Florida State football history is clear: He's the quarterback who passed the 1994 Seminoles to a 31–31 victory over the hated Florida Gators. No, that's not a typographical error. Both teams scored 31 points.

Kanell and FSU, reeling from a 31–3 deficit late in the third quarter, had been reduced to a quest to save face. "I'm thinking, 'How are we going to keep from getting embarrassed out here?'" Kanell said. So he began performing as if he had nothing left to lose. "The fans were already booing, and I had the attitude that it can't get much worse, so let it fly and make the best of the situation," he said.

He let it fly. And did it again and again. He attempted 22 passes in the fourth quarter. He completed 18 of them for 232 yards. When Rock Preston swept 4 yards for a touchdown with 1:45 remaining, Florida's seemingly insurmountable lead had been carved to 31–30. FSU had climaxed an 84-yard touchdown drive two minutes into the fourth quarter and followed it with 3 more covering 60, 73, and 60 yards.

Offensive coordinator Mark Richt said later, "Before [the last] drive, the [offensive] coaches were deciding exactly what two-point

yard performance on 30 carries against the nation's number one–ranked defense.

But over the next fourteen minutes, UM quarterback Steve Walsh passed for 3 touchdowns on plays that accounted for 148 of his 254 passing yards on the day. FSU defensive coordinator play we wanted to run. Coach Bowden heard us. He came over and said, 'Don't do anything until you get my decision on the two.'"

Given Bowden's reputation, it seemed a certainty he'd go for the win. But after Preston scored, he sent out the kicking team. His thinking was twofold: First, 1:45 remained, and he also counted on Spurrier having Danny Wuerffel bomb away. That raised the possibility of an interception or a Florida three-and-out taking little time off the clock. "You knew darned well Steve Spurrier was not going to sit on the ball," Bowden said. But the larger issue, he added, was that he didn't want FSU's gritty rally to go unrewarded. Later, players endorsed the uncharacteristic move. "We got to [31–30] by a miracle," linebacker Todd Rebol reasoned. "If we'd gone for 2 and missed, it would have been the great comeback that almost happened."

As it turned out, the Seminoles did get the ball back, but with only 22 seconds left. The last of those ran out as Kanell scrambled to the Florida 43 yard line. But you could read in the expression of every coach or player who left the field that day that the 31–31 tie had a winner and a loser.

Footnote: The Sugar Bowl arranged a rematch in New Orleans. FSU won what was billed as "the fifth quarter," 23–17.

Mickey Andrews observed, "We had three major mistakes and they came away with 23 points." Walsh's 73-yard hookup with All-America Michael Irvin suddenly staked Miami to a 26–19 lead with 2:22 left in the game.

Safety Dedrick Dodge, victimized with cornerback Martin

Mayhew on that breakdown, later observed that momentum in the fourth quarter shifted so quickly that "It was like someone turned the lights off and turned them back on."

Typifying FSU futility, quarterback McManus fumbled a second-down-and-one snap from Miami's 17 yard line when the Seminoles appeared poised to break back on top from a 19–19 tie several plays before the Walsh-Irvin bombshell. Then in the ensuing scramble, he inadvertently kicked the ball 6 yards upfield straight into the arms of UM safety Bennie Blades.

Schmidt, meanwhile, had endured a nightmarish perform-ance in a wind-buffeted game. FSU's all-time leading scorer mis-fired on two short field goals and also on an extra point he swears was accurate, all subsequent to the Keystone Kops center snap. ("Our signal is 'set,' and Marty Riggs then waits a second and snaps it," Schmidt explained. Whoever yelled "set," it wasn't McManus or Schmidt, who weren't even positioned when the ball rifled past and bounded toward midfield.) Still, after Irvin's go-ahead score, McManus grittily generated an answering touch-down drive, and a pair of time-outs preceded the make-or-break two-point conversion attempt.

FSU's kicking team was trotting onto the field as McManus came toward the sideline after an FSU time-out. "A couple guys running onto the field said, 'Tell him to go for 2,'" McManus said later. That was Bowden's intent anyway. But McManus's lob toward 6–5 tight end Pat Carter was short, and UM safety Bubba McDowell batted it down.

McManus and company had achieved 25 first downs to Miami's 11, outgained the Hurricanes 426 yards to 306, and spent more than forty of the game's sixty minutes on offense. And all FSU had to show for that was the taste of ashes. Bowden called it "one of those 'Why me?' games."

The taste was no less bitter four years later, when Thomas's 34-yard field-goal attempt strayed inches outside the right upright to doom the Seminoles to a 17–16 defeat after they had nursed a 16–7 lead into the fourth quarter. FSU's defense had sacked quarterback Gino Torretta six times in another tour de force. But Torretta maintained his poise and drilled what proved to be a decisive fourth-down-and-six pass from FSU's 12 yard line to wide receiver Horace Copeland for 9 yards and a first down with just over three minutes remaining. That became prelude to the 1-yard touchdown plunge by Larry Jones and a Carlos Huerta extra point that snapped the 16–16 tie.

As in 1987, FSU mounted an answering drive as eventual Heisman Trophy runner-up Weldon moved his troops 63 yards to Miami's 17 yard line. Bowden sent Thomas onto the field for the field-goal attempt with 29 seconds remaining. The twenty-year-old walk-on missed, narrowly.

"I knew it was going to be close because it kept fading," said Thomas, who appeared in shock after the game and needed a few minutes of isolation to compose himself. Holder Brad Johnson said Thomas hit the ball even more solidly than on three previous field-goal successes but that the kick was "1 foot off the whole way."

If a curse truly existed, the NCAA contributed to it. The same kick a year earlier would have made FSU a winner. Between the 1990 and 1991 seasons, NCAA rules makers had narrowed the goal posts from 23 feet 4 inches the previous season to 18 feet 6 inches.

Ever since, "wide right" has been an albatross, starting with Dan Mowrey's misplaced 39-yard bid for a 19–19 tie in 1992, Matt Munyon's 49-yard failure to forge a 27–27 tie and force overtime in 2000, Xavier Beitia's 43-yard miss (this one wide left) on the final snap of a 28–27 FSU loss in 2002, and Beitia's less dramatic but no less decisive failure from 39 yards out with five and a half minutes remaining in UM's 16–14 Orange Bowl victory in a rematch from the 2003 regular season.

The series has not been without periodic joy for FSU. But even a 1989 victory didn't exact the vengeance that would exorcise all demons. Why not? Because FSU won, but Miami, in 24–10 defeat, went on to collect another national championship trophy.

Quarterback Peter Tom Willis was not engaging in empty rhetoric when he said, "I think everybody in the country at the end of the season would admit we were the best . . . From the point where we beat Miami and Auburn back to back, we didn't think anybody could beat us."

That quote was used routinely by those who cover the national scene. FSU finished on a ten-game winning streak culminating in a 41–17 rout of Nebraska in the Fiesta Bowl. But there was no expunging a 30–26 loss to Southern Mississippi and a 34–23 setback against Clemson to start the season.

The victory over Miami featured a 99-yard FSU drive directed by Willis and capped by tailback Amp Lee's 1-yard run to pad a 14–10 lead in the third quarter. It largely resulted from 6 Miami turnovers and a superhuman performance by FSU linebacker Kirk Carruthers, who intercepted 2 passes, forced 1 fumble, and recovered another. And it starred a back who rushed for

142 yards on 21 carries but attracted as much attention for a penalty.

Dexter Carter launched FSU toward victory with an early 37-yard sweep to a touchdown. But the lingering memory of Carter that day involved his reaction to a clipping penalty early in the second half. UM's Roland Smith intercepted a Willis pass, and on the return Hurricanes linebacker Bernard Clark drew a flag for a potentially injurious clip on Carter. The yellow hanky dropped near both players. Carter, infuriated, scooped up the flag, stalked Clark toward the UM sideline, and attempted to stuff it in his facemask. In doing so he dislodged Clark's helmet, and the flag ended up on Clark's shaved head. Carter's unsportsmanlike conduct penalty offset the clipping infraction.

"I lost my poise," Carter said afterwards. "And I did it at the worst possible time. It could have turned momentum totally their way. I apologized to my teammates." The show of temper was unseemly. But still the visual was pretty hilarious.

The wounds inflicted by Miami in 1991 were reopened in 1992 when Mowrey, with a chance to salvage a tie, added his name to the chapter on kicking infamy. Clairvoyantly, he acknowledged the historic implications in the locker room afterwards when he asked disgustedly, "Why did it have to be wide right? Geez!"

In the adjacent locker room in the Orange Bowl stadium, exultant UM linebacker Michael Barrow gloated. "I knew he was going to miss," he said. "We figured they'd choke." Barrow also had loudly questioned FSU's heart as he celebrated on the field. The Seminoles didn't forget.

Before the 1993 meeting, yet another showdown between unbeatens, with FSU ranked number one and Miami number three, FSU fullback William Floyd bristled at the memory of the previous year's game. He recalled that as Mowrey lined up for the field goal, he saw Barrow "and half the rest of their team on their knees praying. Then they come after the game saying we have no heart. Because a kick was missed?"

The aftertaste motivated the Seminoles. But even when they had a 21–10 lead in the fourth quarter, history dictated that they not drop their guard. As Bowden had learned the hard way, and repeated almost as a mantra, "Never, never, never count Miami out."

But this time FSU safety Devin Bush, a Miami native, delivered a knockout blow with 5:40 remaining. He read Frank Costa's eyes as the UM quarterback dropped into the pocket on a third-down-and-five snap. He darted into the path of the pass and returned the interception 40 yards to secure a 28–10 victory.

Bush delivered a message simply by tugging off his sweat-drenched number 11 garnet jersey in the midst of a celebration of the victory that helped deliver FSU's long-overdue national championship. On the T-shirt underneath, he had taken a black Magic Marker, outlined a heart over where the real thing was beating, and filled it in.

## Geniuses at Work

Anyone who questions Steve Spurrier's Xs-and-Os creativity and genius on the attack has probably had his objectivity clouded by the psychological machinations of this intensely competitive coach, who is known equally for his barbed wit.

However, in some respects, Bobby Bowden and Florida State have represented a thorn in Spurrier's flank as aggravating as the one Miami has jabbed into FSU's hide over the years. Bowden always refrained from engaging in the verbal sniping that factored prominently into Spurrier's combative approach. But results of their fourteen jousts from opposing sidelines favored FSU's affable leader.

Spurrier, the 1966 Heisman Trophy winner, arrived back at his alma mater in 1990 and promptly triggered the revival of a sleeping-giant program that had become a portrait of mediocrity the previous four seasons. He shocked the Gator Nation twelve heralded seasons later, when he resigned to confront a new challenge as coach of the NFL's Washington Redskins.

Fortunately, his Florida career will not be defined by his record against Bowden. During Spurrier's tenure, Florida State celebrated eight victories, bemoaned five losses, and reveled in a storybook 31–31 tie that prompted a Sugar Bowl rematch that FSU won.

Spurrier the coach never raised a fist in victory on FSU turf. That 1994 tie, in fact, undoubtedly ranks with the most painful of defeats in his extraordinary career. (The Seminoles erased a 31–3 deficit with a 28-point fourth quarter.) By contrast, Bowden's two victories at Florida Field in the 1990s preceded national-title coronations.

Looking back, the third play of "Bowden-Spurrier I" in 1990 may have set a tone not only for the explosive 45–30 FSU victory that resulted but for a decade-plus in which Spurrier always was playing catch-up in a coaching rivalry he made highly personal. Bowden recognized the significance of that first chess match with

Spurrier. "Any time there's a coaching change—at Florida, Florida State, or Miami, doesn't matter who it is—momentum is going to swing that way [initially]," he said. With Spurrier at the controls, he forecast, the Gators were "back where they ought to be. It's fixing to get back to a three-school race [in the state] again."

Spurrier's first Gators team arrived at Doak Campbell Stadium sporting a 9–1 record and number six national ranking, flaunting a defense that had allowed more than 15 points only twice all season, and pursuing the first ten-victory season in a Florida football history dating back to 1906.

But Casey Weldon took FSU's second snap on the game's first series, rolled to his right, and hurled a perfect strike more than 50 yards to the fingertips of Lawrence Dawsey, who was sprinting down the opposite sideline. The 76-yard touchdown play on which Dawsey did not have to break stride staked the Seminoles to a 7–0 lead with only 57 seconds lapsed. The fireworks display continued for the next fifty-nine entertaining minutes. "The big play to Dawsey must have been the tone-setter," Weldon observed afterwards, "because they did just as well as we did numbers-wise. The key tonight was not turning the ball over. We didn't make mistakes, and they couldn't catch us."

It wasn't for lack of effort or efficiency. Florida quarterback Shane Matthews completed 29 of 48 passes for 351 yards and 2 scores. But the climb always was uphill because of Weldon and All-America Dawsey, who teamed for a 71-yard bookend play of sorts that set up tailback Amp Lee's third touchdown from 2 yards out and provided the Seminoles with a fourth-quarter cushion. Spurrier conceded, "I didn't think any team in the country could move the ball on us the way they did." The Seminoles outgained the Gators, 487 yards to 484, in a classic shoot-out.

When quarterback Charlie Ward and FSU dealt Florida a 33–21 loss in Gainesville three years later, Bowden enjoyed a 3–1 advantage over Spurrier. That victory propelled the Seminoles toward Bowden's first national title. But it was one he did not get to enjoy for long; Spurrier inflicted part of the pain and injected a caustic undercurrent into an already emotional rivalry.

*Sports Illustrated* exposed a $6,000 shopping spree at a Tallahassee Foot Locker store in May 1994 to which unscrupulous sports agents—you sometimes wonder if there is any other kind—treated a number of FSU football players. Even as FSU president Sandy D'Alemberte engaged in damage control by taking a proactive stance and hiring an independent law firm to investigate, Spurrier was delighting Gators booster clubs with jabs about "Free Shoes University." Disingenuously, he hinted that coaches and alumni were subsidizing FSU players when he said, "Maybe we're realizing why they signed so many of those top players." In reprimanding Spurrier, University of Florida President John Lombardi made oblique reference to the fact the NCAA twice in the 1980s placed the UF program on probation for infractions.

Spurrier's baiting of not only FSU but also Southeastern Conference rivals Tennessee, Auburn, and Georgia usually was couched in humor. "You go to booster or quarterback clubs, and you generally want to say something that the people would like to hear," was the way he rationalized his quest to entertain Florida fans at a rival's expense. But that was neither the first or last time he took razor-edged swipes at Bowden and his program.

Bowden was embarrassed not only by the Foot Locker

episode but also by a rash of off-field transgressions of varying seriousness by players. Minor missteps added to the perception of a major problem. Most involved poor judgment by teenagers. This was not a program infected by bad actors. For an example, among those suspended for from two to four 1994 games in the Foot Locker aftermath was All-America linebacker Derrick Brooks, whose charitable works since as a pro long ago erased any questions about his extraordinary strength of character.

Undeniable is the fact that the Foot Locker episode, for which FSU eventually received a one-year probation without sanctions, brought positive change. D'Alemberte's efforts forced FSU to revisit how it educates its athletes to deal with agents; they also turned a harsh spotlight on the plague sports agents inflict on all major programs nationally and resulted in state statutes under which agents became subject to prosecution.

Ironically, Florida became the focus when an agent named William "Tank" Black was sentenced to a one-year jail term and a substantial fine for wooing several Gator players, including defensive end Jevon Kearse, with monthly payments of up to $500 during the 1998 season.

Bowden's record against Spurrier stood at 4–2–1 when Spurrier brought the nation's number one–ranked Gators to Tallahassee to play the number two Seminoles in a 1996 battle of unbeatens, and this game precipitated yet another exercise in vitriol.

Danny Wuerffel, who weeks later would accept the Heisman Trophy, had difficulty coping not only with flag-snapping 20-mile-per-hour winds that made passes sail like Frisbees but also with a punishing FSU defense bent on rattling him. Wuerffel doesn't rattle. But at game's end, the Gators were on the short end of a 24–21 score, and FSU, which vaulted to a 17–0 lead and held on, was the new number one.

Warrick Dunn did much of the damage for FSU. He rushed for 185 yards, caught passes for 24 more, and even completed a pass for 10. Tackle Todd Fordham said in awe, "He's unreal. Warrick Dunn shows up for big games like no other player in the world." But Dunn's heroics did not stay in the headlines for long. Spurrier commanded those.

All-America end Peter Boulware undoubtedly fueled the Florida coach's subsequent charges that the Seminoles played dirty when he said beforehand, "The only way to stop Wuerffel is to make sure he's on his back with the ball." Though Wuerffel did connect on 23 of 48 passes for 362 yards and 3 touchdowns, he also suffered 3 interceptions—and absorbed a brutal beating. The Seminoles shredded a patchwork offensive line to sack Wuerffel six times and put him on the ground another twenty-five times, give or take a couple bruises.

Officials did flag the Seminoles for 143 yards in penalties, including two for roughing the passer. But postgame comments did not foretell the storm Spurrier would stir over the next few days. Spurrier's game-day summation was that "when you ask your quarterback to make fifty or sixty plays, you're going to have some bad ones. Danny took a beating in the first half."

FSU defensive coordinator Mickey Andrews, who became the primary unnamed target of Spurrier's subsequent diatribes, said in the winner's locker room, "We knew going in we were not going to shut those guys down [totally]. Danny Wuerffel's got to be as good as there is, maybe ever."

The tenor changed, however, after Spurrier dissected game

film, spewed invective at the FSU players and staff, and had a video made of eight plays including the two roughing-the-passer infractions. The controversy took on an extended shelf life one week later when Texas aborted what shaped up as a Florida State–Nebraska Sugar Bowl by shocking the once-beaten Cornhuskers, 37–27. Suddenly a Florida-FSU rematch resurrected an improbable but possible national championship for Spurrier's Gators. National media who witnessed Spurrier's video in New Orleans appeared to react with a collective "that's Steve" smile and a "that's football" shrug. One I questioned acknowledged the roughing penalties and said one or two more of the hits might have been borderline.

Longtime FSU assistant Jim Gladden, who tutored a parade of All-America defensive ends, at least outwardly dismissed Spurrier's rant: "There's always an agenda when anything's said. It might be to motivate his players. It might be to distract ours. Who knows what it is?"

The reaction outside Florida possibly was tempered by the recognition that Spurrier's "fun 'n gun" offense routinely exposed his quarterbacks to a pounding. Never was that more evident than a year earlier, when Nebraska and a group of fleet outside linebackers battered Wuerffel throughout a 62–24 Fiesta Bowl with the national championship on the line. The Cornhuskers' defensive brain trust undoubtedly studied film of a 35–24 Florida victory over FSU—achieved despite 7 sacks of Wuerffel. The Huskers' Fiesta romp also featured 7 sacks, 4 of those including

*Defensive end Peter Boulware was all over Florida's Danny Wuerffel throughout the Seminoles' 24–21 victory in 1996.*

a safety in a 29–0 second quarter that made the second half super-fluous.

Spurrier's scheme relied on snap decisions by the quarter-back but sacrificed pass protection for the opportunity to put more receivers into the pattern. The idea was that a linebacker or blitzing defensive back rushing from the flank wouldn't be quick enough to get to Wuerffel before the ball was gone. But those at FSU and Nebraska were quick enough.

Spurrier's revenge, and his only back-to-back victories over Bowden, followed the 24–21 loss at Tallahassee and deprived the Seminoles of one national championship and probably two.

In the Sugar Bowl rematch, a 52–20 romp that established beyond any reasonable doubt that Florida was the better team, Spurrier swallowed his distaste for the shotgun formation to give Wuerffel a longer read on FSU's defenses and also fortified pass protection. This capitalized not only on Wuerffel's poise and accuracy but also on the elusiveness of spotlighted receivers Rei-del Anthony and Ike Hilliard. Anthony had expressed frustration after the 24–21 loss. "If [Wuerrfel] had had more time, we would have killed them," he said. "I was getting behind [secondary defenders] all day. Their defensive backs weren't that good."

The rematch supported his contention. Wuerffel passed for 360 yards and 3 touchdowns. It's true that the game didn't become a rout until severe cramping, an offshoot of a weeklong battle with the flu, sent an ailing Dunn to the locker room for good with FSU down only 24–20 early in the second half. But the Gators had been energized by a 20–17 Ohio State victory over Jake Plummer and previously unbeaten Arizona State in the Rose Bowl the night before, and that resurrected their shot at what became Spurrier's only national championship. They deserved it, especially Wuerffel, who throughout the furor over "dirty football" took the high road in his remarks.

Ten months later Florida State arrived in Gainesville sporting a 10–0 record and a number two ranking behind Michigan. Spurrier crossed up his rival by alternating quarterbacks Doug Johnson and Noah Brindise on practically every play. Some will tell you to this day that the 1966 Heisman Trophy winner never "quarterbacked" a better game. Still, it took a 63-yard pass play, Johnson to Jacquez Green, to set up tailback Fred Taylor's fourth touchdown. A 1-yard plunge with 1:50 remaining erased a 29–25 Florida deficit.

Samari Rolle, the talented senior cornerback whom Green beat on his long gain, was almost inconsolable. He bemoaned "ruined" dreams and aspirations and the fact "all the Gator jokes directed at us . . . I'll have no way to ever come back [at them]."

Over in Florida's locker room, Taylor, who had rushed for 162 yards, referenced Florida's earlier losses to Louisiana State and Georgia that season when he said happily, "It means [the Seminoles] can't go to the national championship game if I can't go."

And have the agony and the ecstasy in those two reactions ever better defined rivalry?

# Exercise in Brinksman-ship

What if some Game Boy whiz decided to computerize an eight-team tournament for truly rabid Florida State fans to determine the best of the university's thirty-years-and-counting Bobby Bowden era? The entry list naturally would start with the 1999 Seminoles, who carried the number one national ranking from green flag to checkered and achieved 12–0 perfection with the 46–29 Sugar Bowl victory over Virginia Tech in a battle of unbeatens. It would also feature the 1993 national champions who overcame a loss at Notre Dame and dealt previously unbeaten Nebraska a nerve-grinding 18–16 defeat in the Orange Bowl.

But there would be no shortage of talented teams between 1979 and 2000 to fill the bracket, spice the elimination rounds, and provide stiff competition for the Chris Weinke– and Charlie Ward–directed outfits that achieved their ultimate goal. Here they are in chronological order.

**1979 season (11–1).** A defense that featured All-America nose tackle Ron Simmons permitted only 136 points in an 11–0 regular season before Barry Switzer's Oklahoma Sooners dealt the Seminoles a 24–7 Orange Bowl loss. Quarterback J .C. Watts and Heisman Trophy–winning tailback Billy Sims each rushed for more than 100 yards to squelch the dreams of a team that rocket-boosted FSU's national profile.

**1980 season (10–2).** A pair of 1-point losses, 10–9 at Miami and 18–17 against Oklahoma in an Orange Bowl rematch, deprived FSU of a perfect season. But those did not diminish the long-term impact of an 18–14 victory at Nebraska built on frenetic linebacker play by Paul Piurowski and Reggie Herring. Nor did they erase a 36–22 triumph that would spoil an otherwise perfect season for a Pittsburgh team that featured sophomore quarterback Dan Marino and, in defensive tackle Hugh Green and offensive tackle Mark May, showcased the Lombardi and Outland Award winners. Pitt finished with a number two ranking behind champion Georgia and Heisman-winning tailback Her-

# Nice Hit, Michael

Chris Weinke's six seasons in the Toronto Blue Jays' farm system didn't get him to the major leagues. But he'll always have fond memories and stories to tell, like the night in Birmingham, Alabama, when he was playing first base for Class AA Knoxville.

A Barons rookie, hitless in his first seven at-bats as a professional and a strikeout victim in five of those, singled early in the game. Weinke recalled years later, "He said he'd better get the baseball because he didn't know if he'd ever get another hit." In fact, the rookie singled again later in the game. But his baseball career proved to be a brief sabbatical from the sport that made him one of the world's most famous athletes. Michael Jordan eventually went back to collect more National Basketball Association championship rings.

By the way, Weinke wisely invested the $375,000 bonus with which Toronto enticed him off the Florida State campus in the summer of 1990 in real estate and stocks and bonds.

Tailback Travis Minor playfully observed that when Weinke returned to FSU in his mid-twenties, he fit right in—with an asterisk. "Everybody talks about his age, but he relates to the [other] players just like he's our age. He's one of us." Except . . . "The main difference is that everybody else around here is broke."

schel Walker. Seven of FSU's ten victims scored 7 or fewer points; only Pitt, in defeat, and Oklahoma exceeded 14.

**1987 season (11–1).** The University of Miami, though thoroughly dominated early, overcame a 19–3 deficit to take a 26–19 lead on quarterback Steve Walsh's third touchdown pass, a 72-yard hookup with Michael Irvin with 2:22 left. FSU quarterback Danny McManus directed an answering touchdown march in the waning seconds, but UM's Bubba McDowell batted down McManus's underthrown two-point conversion pass as Bowden went for the victory. The Seminoles' average winning margin in the ten regular-season victories was 30.6 points, and among victims were Big Ten champion Michigan State and Southeastern Conference co-champion Auburn.

**1988 season (11–1).** An overconfident bunch that made an ill-advised rap video during the off-season and then absorbed a 31–0 beating at Miami in the opener never lost again. Those Seminoles crushed their final eight regular-season victims by an average of 33.6 points. A sloppy 13–7 Sugar Bowl victory over Auburn was sealed when cornerback Deion Sanders, on his final play of his final game at FSU, intercepted a Reggie Slack pass in the end zone with 5 seconds remaining.

**1989 season (10–2).** Southern Mississippi quarterback Bret Favre passed 2 yards to tight end Anthony Harris with 23 seconds remaining in the season opener to saddle FSU with a 30–26 loss. A week later Clemson and tailback Terry Allen sent the Seminoles reeling to 0–2 with a 34–23 victory in Tallahassee. Had FSU won either game, it would have won the national championship. That's indisputable because among the ten consecutive victories that followed was a 24–10 whipping of Miami—and Miami won the national championship.

**1991 season (11–2).** Casey Weldon quarterbacked the Seminoles to a 10–0 start, all victories by double digits, and positioned Gerry Thomas for a winning 34-yard field goal against Miami. But Thomas's misfire launched the "wide right" history of the series with the Hurricanes. FSU lost, 17–16, and followed with a listless effort in a 14–9 defeat at Florida.

**1996 season (11–1).** This was the team from which NFL scouts snatched four first-rounders among the first fourteen picks in the 1997 draft: defensive ends Peter Boulware and Reinard Wilson, tailback Warrick Dunn, and offensive tackle Walter Jones. It was a team that capped an 11–0 regular season with a home-field 24–21 victory over Florida and Heisman-winning quarterback Danny Wuerffel, only to have subsequent developments force a Sugar Bowl rematch. The superior Gators won, 52–20, with 28–3 second-half dominance after the departure of a flu-stricken and cramping Dunn.

**2000 season (11–2).** This Weinke-propelled team retained a controversial shot at the national championship against Oklahoma in the Orange Bowl despite a 27–24 regular-season loss to Miami on the same turf. It was a team that scored 514 points and allowed only 133, a statistical superiority exceeded only by the 1993 champions' 536–129 cumulative margin.

That adds up to ten teams. A couple more would not have been out of place among those bidding for "playoff" berths. Identifying the entrants by quarterback and year, a case also could be made for the Ward/1992 and Thad Busby/1997 teams.

To get down to eight, scratch Weldon/1991 because of that team's limping finish and Chip Ferguson/1988 because of a succession of pushover opponents after the 31–0 loss at Miami and the 24–21 "puntrooskie" survival at Clemson.

Seeding largely on the basis of record, and recognizing the utter subjectivity of conclusions, the quarterfinals might shake out this way:

No. 1 Weinke/1999 eliminates No. 8 Jimmy Jordan/1979
No. 2 Ward/1993 eliminates No. 7 Weinke/2000
No. 6 Rick Stockstill/1980 upsets No. 3 Busby/1996
No. 4 McManus/1987 eliminates No. 5 Willis/1989

Other than to shake the FSU family tree for great memories and stir predictable debate, the more pertinent point of this entire exercise follows with these semifinals:

No. 2 Ward/1993 outpoints No. 6 Stockstill/1980
No. 4 McManus/1987 upsets No. 1 Weinke/1999

In their lone loss against Miami, those 1987 Seminoles were like a heavyweight who fashions a masterful and artistic performance only to get nailed by a haymaker in the final round. Otherwise, on their best day and because McManus seemed to have a magic touch, I'd rank that team a close runner-up only to the Ward/1993 champions who offset the loss at Notre Dame with victories over five teams—including number three Nebraska and number four Florida—that retained top-twenty-five rankings after the bowls.

The bottom line is, the one Bowden team that skated through a season without defeat may have been no better than his third- or fourth-best . . . and that can be flipped like a flapjack to reflect that any team that can survive as many close calls as Weinke and Company did warrants greater admiration than any of the others.

The Seminoles survived a 41–35 shoot-out with Georgia Tech, fought to a 21–21 halftime tie with Miami before prevailing, and, remarkably, trailed in the second half in four of their final five victories. This would have been great grist for one of those 1950s movie serials that always left the heroine hanging from the cliff by her fingertips or tied to railroad tracks from one Saturday to the next. A review is in order.

## FSU 41, Georgia Tech 35

Joe Hamilton, the quarterback and catalyst for a team coming off a 10–2 season, kept the Seminoles on their heels throughout a 945-yard shoot-out. Not until Travis Minor cradled an onside kick with 1:35 remaining did the Seminoles breathe a collective sigh of relief. "I don't want to play one more second of that game," Bowden said afterwards. "It has been a long time since I've seen us get pushed around on defense like that."

"The only thing we didn't do," Hamilton said, "was win the game . . . We feel we can make plays against anyone in the country." Incredibly, FSU marched to touchdowns on four consecutive possessions in the first half, and Georgia Tech answered the first three with touchdown drives of their own. That's seven possessions, seven touchdowns.

Hamilton, a 5'10" dervish with the versatility of Charlie Ward, not only operated Tech's option efficiently but completed 22 of 25 passes for 387 yards and 4 touchdowns. "To complete 22 of 25 passes . . ." marveled FSU assistant head coach Chuck Amato, "that's hard to do in practice when you're throwing against *nothing*." Indeed Hamilton was shredding a unit that included seven returning starters from college football's stingiest defense the year before.

But Weinke and mates converted eight of fourteen third-down plays for first downs when any misplay might have reversed fortunes. Weinke completed 16 of 25 passes for 262 yards and 3 touchdowns, Peter Warrick had 8 receptions for 142 yards, and thunderfoot Sebastian Janikowski provided the winning margin with second-half field goals of 46 and 45 yards.

## FSU 31, Miami 21

A week of turmoil precipitated by the arrests of receivers Peter Warrick and Laveranues Coles for their roles in a Dillard's department store scam preceded the annual showdown against Miami. Warrick was suspended, Coles subsequently was kicked off the team, and the prospect of a Seminole letdown loomed. "Now we find out if we've got a team," a subdued Bowden said.

But linebacker Brian Allen dismissed the notion of a collapse, pointing out, "Weinke's still there. He's the general of the offense."

UM quarterback Kenny Kelly had a magnificent first half. He launched 3 touchdown passes, 2 to Santana Moss and 1 to Reggie

Wayne, as the Hurricanes shot out to a 21–14 lead before the mid-point of the second quarter. But FSU's defense cracked down, shutting out the 'Canes over the final forty minutes and allowing only one successful third-down conversion after halftime.

Meanwhile, Weinke found eleven different receivers with his 23 pass completions for 332 yards, and tailback Travis Minor's 25-carry, 146-yard costarring role featured a 47-yard gallop that helped set up Janikowski's tie-breaking field goal in the third quarter.

Moss, who produced 180 yards with 9 receptions in the losing effort, said after UM's fifth consecutive loss in the streaky series, "We showed our character today, and Florida State showed us they don't need Peter Warrick to win."

They would two weeks later.

# FSU 17, Clemson 14

University officials cleared Warrick to play at Clemson some twenty-four hours before kickoff after he pleaded guilty to charges properly reduced from felony grand theft to misdemeanor petty theft in the Dillard's episode that involved some $400 in clothing.

It didn't appear that would prevent Tommy Bowden's Tigers from stunning Papa Bowden's Seminoles after whirling-dervish quarterback Woodrow Dantzler directed Clemson to a 14–3 half-time advantage. Tommy even emulated his father's early-career propensity for trick plays when punter Ryan Romano passed 23 yards to Braxton Williams to keep alive a scoring drive.

*Bobby Bowden's three hundredth victory came at the expense of son Tommy (Clemson's coach) in the first father-son coaching matchup in college football history.*

Poor Ann Bowden. Not only was this a historic first matchup between teams coached by a father and son, but a victory would be the three hundredth for her husband. Tommy Bowden coached Tulane to a perfect season the year before but brought a 3–3 Clemson team into the civil war. Ann Bowden wanted her son's new team to perform well, but her husband's team had much more riding on the outcome.

The prospect of an FSU defeat began to dawn on her as she stifled her emotions in the stands. "It didn't start to hit me until the third quarter," she said when she joined her husband for the postgame press conference. "I thought, 'That's enough, Tommy.'"

Weinke, again justifying teammates' belief that the "old man" would bring them back, directed a 12-play, 51-yard drive to a 33-yard field goal by Janikowski to trim Clemson's lead to 14–6 early in the third quarter. He then completed 3 of his 4 passes in a 10-play, 68-yard push culminating in Minor's 2-yard touchdown run and forged a 14–14 tie with a two-point pass to fullback Dan Kendra.

Janikowki's decisive 39-yard field goal with 5:30 left in the game capped a 58-yard drive for a 17–14 lead that held up only after cornerback Tay Cody barely deflected a 41-yard field-goal attempt by Clemson freshman Tony Lazzara with 1:57 remaining.

Warrick, subjected to fan harassment that became commonplace, finished the night with 11 receptions for 121 yards. But, uncharacteristically, he also dropped four catchable balls in a show of rust. "When you practice two days out of three weeks," Bowden said of the two-week suspension while legal issues were settled, "that's the result you usually get."

Victory number three hundred wore Bowden out. "You feel you're losing the game. You're going to get beat . . . You're going to get beat . . . You're going to get beat. And all of a sudden you win, and you don't even know how."

# FSU 35, Virginia 10

Chris Weinke endured 3 interceptions in a discombobulated first half that ended with ambitious Virginia on top, 10–7.

"I'm getting a first-half complex," Bowden said. A 71-yard escape that led to a field goal contributed to a 164-yard performance by tailback Thomas Jones, who entered as the number two rusher in Division 1-A with a 158.4-yards-per-game average.

Nose tackle Corey Simon (left) raises the national championship trophy to his lips in celebration of a 46–29 victory over Virginia Tech.

But as it had previously against Miami and Clemson, coordinator Mickey Andrews's defense pitched a second-half shutout, this one with the help of a diving interception by All-America nose tackle Corey Simon as he dropped into pass coverage on a zone-blitz call.

Said Bowden, "I'm just amazed at how our defensive coaches go in and make halftime adjustments and come out and shut teams down, game after game, year after year." Clemson had netted a mere 70 yards after intermission. Virginia managed only 103.

The second half became a rout as Weinke, again drawing on the maturity expected of a twenty-seven-year-old, shook off early travails to complete 12 of his final 16 passes in a 297-yard, 3-touchdown performance.

Virginia coach George Welsh observed of the Seminoles, "They have a pretty good knack of turning it up a notch in the second half. [They take] over the game on defense first to enable their offense to get going."

## FSU 30, Florida 23

Two years previously, an unbeaten, number one–ranked Florida State team had rolled into Gainesville only to have coach Steve Spurrier's Gators pull off a 32–29 upset. Then, Florida receiver Jacquez Green had maneuvered past cornerback Samari Rolle to snare Doug Johnson's perfect pass and turn it into a 63-yard pickup to FSU's 17 yard line late in the game. Fred Taylor followed with a 16-yard burst and then the fourth touchdown of his sensational 162-yard performance from a yard out with only 1:50 left.

Spurrier's manipulation of alternating quarterbacks Johnson and Noah Brindise drew rave reviews, and he reverted to that pattern again in the 1999 showdown. The strategy may have backfired. The Gators' offense, with Johnson and Jesse Palmer sharing the duty, did net 442 yards but misfired with penalties and misplays at critical moments. "We played pretty close to give-away ball today," Spurrier said. "It was embarrassing."

Still FSU won because Weinke didn't flinch after an interception that presented the Gators with a 16–13 lead midway through the third quarter. Bennie Alexander returned the theft 43 yards to shift momentum to Florida and send Gators fans into a deafening frenzy that continued into the next possession.

"But Chris follows mistakes with great plays," Bowden said. "That goes back to maturity." Weinke immediately engineered a 52-yard drive climaxed by a tying 54-yard field goal by Janikowski. First Janikowski drilled a 49-yarder. A delay penalty nullified the kick, so he calmly returned to nail the 54-yarder.

Tommy Polley's punt block set FSU up for a 21-yard go-ahead drive, and Weinke directed a subsequent 78-yard scoring assault in only five snaps. He passed 38 yards to Warrick along the way and connected with Marvin Minnis for 27 yards and the touchdown. In all, Weinke completed 8 of his 10 passes after the interception. "I never felt worried," he said, "even when I threw the interception."

Even so, Palmer was sending a "Hail, Mary" into the end zone on the final snap, and Spurrier concluded, "The '97 team was a lot better than the team they have now, in my opinion."

# FSU 46, Virginia Tech 29

Weinke's fourth-quarter rescue mission and Warrick's spectacular FSU finale in the national championship Sugar Bowl are perhaps the highlight of FSU's football legacy. But the manner in which Weinke brought the Seminoles back from a 29–28 deficit with a sparkling 18-point fourth quarter fit the by-then-established pattern of perils survived.

It was after the 31–21 victory over Miami that a clairvoyant Weinke observed, "Any time you have obstacles or controversies, how you overcome those can be really the potion for team success." None of his FSU-record 650 pass completions ever hit a target more squarely.

# Trickery, Pterodactyls, and Tradition

College football raconteur Beano Cook called it "the best play since *My Fair Lady*." He would get no debate from those left slack-jawed by the call and the execution at Memorial Stadium in Clemson, South Carolina, that idyllic Saturday in September 1988. "Puntrooskie" will reign forever as the boldest and riskiest of the multitude of trick plays Bobby Bowden's Florida State football teams have attempted because it probably was born of the greatest desperation.

A fake punt? On fourth down from your own 21 yard line? In a 21–21 game? With 1:33 remaining? Against the nation's number three team? On the road? You wouldn't dare.

But Bowden would. And any essay on the most fantastic plays and fascinating games over the two decades of Florida State football from 1981 through 2000 must start with puntrooskie and include the memorable 24–21 victory the Seminoles surfed like a giant wave to an 11–1 season.

"If you're looking for a favorite," Bowden said years later of his grab bag of tricks, "you have to say, 'Which one would you not likely ever try again?' That's the one." He laughed. "I've had too much time to think about what would have happened if it hadn't worked."

What would have happened, in all likelihood, is that Clemson's Chris Gardocki would have kicked a game-winning field goal to deal an FSU team ranked number one before the season its second loss in three games. Miami already had humiliated the Seminoles, 31–0, in the opener. Given great expectations dashed by the compounded agony of defeat, an ensuing collapse would not have been beyond the realm of possibility.

But the Xs moved as orchestrated, and the Os reacted as expected, and a player with a lively wit and a magnetic personality turned the moment into a snatch of history that will have true FSU fans recalling his name and his dash twenty or thirty years from now.

LeRoy Butler didn't win an Oscar or an Emmy or a Golden Globe for his performance. Indeed, in a locker room interview that added to FSU's high hilarity in the aftermath, he said that initially he was reluctant even to take the role. But he carried it off.

Forgive a little embellishment by the junior defensive back who became an All-America cornerback a year later and a six-time Pro Bowl performer during a fourteen-year career with the Green Bay Packers. He heard coaches make the call as he started onto the field with the punting unit. By his playfully exaggerated account, he turned back to ask, "Are you sure you want to run that?" only to be shooed out onto the field. As he trotted into position, he said he was "feeling pressure with a capital P" and sneaked a peak toward the Clemson sideline. He swore he felt as if Clemson coach Danny Ford was staring a hole in him.

So, LeRoy, you had butterflies? "More like pterodactyls," he countered.

Later, asked to describe "puntrooskie," Bowden stood up and giddily started moving chairs around to represent players as he spoke of how he'd first seen the play run by veteran coach Jerry Claiborne but also had watched film of Arkansas State trying it. Here's how it shook out: Center David Whittingham snapped the ball not to punter Tim Corlew but to upback Dayne Williams, while Corlew first leaped as if the ball had sailed over his head and then turned to take up frantic pursuit. That was deception number one.

Williams, positioned behind and to the left of blocking back Butler in the alignment, caught the snap, stepped quickly behind Butler, and slipped the ball between Butler's legs into his waiting hands as he froze in a crouch a couple yards behind the line of scrimmage. "I was nervous," Williams said. "The main thing I wanted to do was not fumble the snap. That would have thrown off all the timing. So I concentrated it into my hands and then put the ball between LeRoy's legs."

Deception number two ensued. Butler's instructions were to freeze in place and count off 3 seconds while Williams did a 270-degree pirouette. In doing so, Williams turned his back so that any Clemson rushers whose attention may have shifted from Corlew to Williams could not see that he did not have the ball. He took flight on an apparent sweep around right end convoyed by pulling guards. Whether Butler completed the count to "one thousand three" is uncertain. But he delayed long enough. Traffic had cleared when he darted alone toward the left sideline and realized the subterfuge was working. "I said, 'Ohmigod! It's open. Go, LeRoy, go,'" he related to laughter.

He was hauled down by All-America cornerback Donnell Woolford 78 yards later, at the Clemson 1-yard line. As it turned out, a Richie Andrews field goal became necessary when officials nullified an apparent 3-yard touchdown play. (Bowden all but assaulted the official who explained to him that because the 25-second clock had not started, it was no play.)

Back to Butler. Was he tired after the 78-yard sprint? "I was *past* tired," he said. In fact, his workload that day included 14 tackles from his safety position. Was he excited? "I'm *past* excited," he replied, grinning. "I couldn't feel no better if I was on an island with ten million women."

As Butler held court, offensive line coach Wayne McDuffie walked by, smiling, and called out to Butler, "We *told* you we were going to make you a hero." Nobody, however, was more

All-America cornerback LeRoy Butler will be best remembered for his 78-yard "puntrooskie" dash against Clemson in 1988.

confident than defensive line coach Chuck Amato. "On second down I told someone, 'I hope we don't make an inch,'" he said. "I knew we were only going to win with the fake punt."

Bowden hadn't dismissed the idea of a national championship after the fizzle at Miami. But he knew that a loss and a tie would dash whatever sliver of hope remained as decisively as a second loss. He also knew that Clemson, which lost only once more in a 10–2 season and finished number nine in the Associated Press poll, posed a challenge that might require a joker in his deck.

Clemson already had slipped a joker from its own sleeve, with an end-around leading to receiver Chip Davis's 61-yard touchdown pass to receiver Gary Cooper. The spectacle also featured Deion Sanders's "called-shot," 74-yard punt return to forge a 14–14 tie. He visibly bantered with players on the Clemson sideline as he dropped to field the punt. "Their guys were taunting me, saying, 'Hey, Prime Time, you're nothing. You're no All-American.' Stuff like that," he said. "I said, 'It's going back.'"

But everything that happened before Tim Corlew chased an imaginary ball, Dayne Williams faked a sweep to the right without the ball, and LeRoy Butler took a well-concealed handoff became incidental to the "greatest play since *My Fair Lady*." During the week before FSU's 13–7 Sugar Bowl victory over Auburn climaxed the eleven-game winning streak, a reporter whimsically asked Butler the odds of FSU trotting out punt-rooskie again. "About a million to nothing," he joked.

If you put a gun to my head and force me to rate the five most memorable FSU games I've covered, that classic would have to be one of them. Three others are the 46–29 Sugar Bowl triumph over Virginia Tech for the 1999 national championship, the

33–21 victory at Florida that preserved 1993 title hopes and climaxed with Charlie Ward's dump pass to Warrick Dunn for 79 yards and a touchdown, and Miami's stunning rally for the 26–25 victory in Tallahassee that cost FSU the 1987 national title.

With so much at stake so often and so much history written over such a sensational fourteen-year run, paring the list to five requires splitting hairs. But I can't leave out a mind-boggling 51–31 victory at Michigan in 1991. The showdown between teams ranked number one and number three featured the eventual winners of the Heisman Trophy (Michigan's Desmond Howard), the Davey O'Brien Quarterback Award (Casey Weldon), the Butkus Award (Michigan's Erik Anderson), and the Jim Thorpe Award (Terrell Buckley) . . . not to mention FSU linebacker Marvin Jones, who won both the Butkus Award and the Lombardi Award the next season.

The 106,145 fans who packed Michigan Stadium stands barely had settled into their seats when Buckley baited Michigan quarterback Elvis Grbac into a quick sideline pass toward Howard and darted forward to intercept and stake FSU to a 7–0 lead with a 40-yard touchdown return. The fans never again had time to draw a deep breath and relax before FSU linebacker Howard Dinkins intercepted a 3-yard Grbac pass into the end zone in the final minute of the most thrill-packed half of college football I've ever seen.

I still can picture writers who covered college football for *USA Today*, the *New York Times*, *Sports Illustrated*, and other major publications sitting back and just grinning at what they'd seen as the teams headed for the locker rooms. The score: Florida State 31, Michigan 23.

Three FSU quarterbacks had completed passes to that point: Weldon 10 for 160 yards and a touchdown; Brad Johnson, the holder for placekicks, a shovel pass to fullback/wing blocker William Floyd on a fake field goal that became a 4-yard touchdown; and Charlie Ward (two years before his own Heisman Trophy–winning season) on a throwback pass to Weldon after Ward had lined up at wide receiver to catch a long lateral from Weldon. That double-pass netted 29 yards and led to Johnson's touchdown ruse.

Amazingly by halftime there also had been: (1) a blocked extra-point kick after the Seminoles' successful field-goal fake; (2) another extra-point attempt by FSU's Dan Mowrey that hit the crossbar and bounced back after a 5-yard Amp Lee touchdown run; (3) a 47-yard field goal by Michigan's J. D. Carlson that hit the crossbar and bounced *through*; and (4) failed two-point conversion passes by both Weldon and Grbac. And this extraordinary scene played out during halftime: Former FSU placekicker Richie Andrews, then on the Detroit Lions' taxi squad, worked with punter John Wimberly on extra-point kicks while the University of Michigan band was still performing.

The air didn't exactly go out of the balloon in the second half, but Weldon's touchdown passes to wide receiver Eric Turral (20 yards) and tight end Lonnie Johnson (10 yards) provided a 44–23 cushion that removed all doubt about the outcome. It was almost as if both teams had been drained by the frenzied first half. FSU's 51 points were the most ever scored against the Wolverines on their home field.

The other indelible memory from that day is the Howard-Buckley duel. Howard not only caught 2 touchdown passes but added 60 yards on punt returns and 60 more on kickoff returns. But Buckley intercepted 2 passes and helped limit Howard to 4 receptions for 69 yards. On one Howard score, Buckley tended him so tightly that his arm got trapped beneath Howard's as he moved to knock down the pass.

You could write an entire book about FSU's remarkable showdowns with rivals Miami and Florida. But let me share lasting memories of a few more games that involved neither the Hurricanes nor Gators.

The now-defunct Blockbuster Bowl in Miami's Joe Robbie Stadium matched Joe Paterno and Bobby Bowden, both over sixty by then but still plotting strategy and shaping lives fifteen years later when Penn State and FSU next got together in the Orange Bowl. Their 1990 meeting came during a somewhat disjointed college football season in which no team was dominant. FSU had lost at Miami and at Auburn before a midseason quarterback switch from Brad Johnson to Casey Weldon and entered on a run of five straight victories. Penn State lost at Southern California and at Texas to open the season but had reeled off nine straight victories, including an upset of number one–ranked Notre Dame.

Bowden said before the bowl, "I really believe this: We might be playing the best team in the nation . . . unless Penn State is playing the best team in the nation." Weldon said the Nittany Lions had "plain clothes," Penn State's traditionally unadorned blue or white jerseys in keeping with Paterno's no-frills approach, "but some awesome athletes in them."

But Weldon passed for 248 yards, wide receiver Lawrence Dawsey contributed 8 catches for 107 yards, and tailback Amp

*The friendly rivalry between Bobby Bowden and Joe Paterno continues, but through the 2005 season, Bowden still held the lead in major college football victories.*

Lee earned MVP honors with 86 rushing yards and a pair of touchdowns as FSU prevailed, 24–17.

Then, as now, the Bowdens and Paternos were good friends. Paterno's wife, Suzanne, visited the FSU locker room afterwards to give Bowden a congratulatory hug.

Bowden was euphoric. "That has to be one of the best wins for Florida State," he said. "To me, it's like beating a Notre Dame. That could be because of all the years I spent at West Virginia in the glow of Penn State dominating Eastern football." His head-to-head record against Paterno before the Blockbuster was 0–6.

Bowden also said he had never enjoyed a bowl as much as that one because of the association with Paterno. "When you've beaten Joe, you've accomplished something." (Paterno won their 2006 rematch, a triple-overtime 26–23 Orange Bowl victory played, ironically, in the same stadium as the 24–17 FSU triumph. Both were acclaimed as battles for the ages, and you had to wonder if their teams might meet again when both are in their eighties. Neither icon had yet shown an interest in retiring.)

A game that probably would slip under the radar for most reminiscing about the great ones is a 47–21 FSU victory at Virginia in 1997. But circumstances elevate it for me.

Two years earlier in Charlottesville, Virginia, the Seminoles had suffered their first Atlantic Coast Conference loss after a 29–0 start to league membership. Warrick Dunn's bid for a 6-yard touchdown run on the game's final snap came up bare inches shy of the goal line in the Cavaliers' 33–28 survival.

The entire ACC celebrated. Finally the giant had been slain. FSU, dominant since its 1992 ACC entry, could be beaten after all. And that raised the anticipation for the Seminoles' next visit. The Cavaliers and their fans were pumped. But not for long.

# The Ones That Got Away

Succeed spectacularly enough and often enough, and suddenly cynics tend to judge you as much or more by your losses than by your victories. Only in that context can you make sense of anyone concluding that Bobby Bowden and Florida State have won "only" two national championships.

Five times in the eight seasons between 1993 and 2000, the Seminoles arrived at the site of their bowl within a victory of ruling college football. In 1993 and 1999, they claimed the crown. At the conclusion of the 1996, 1998, and 2000 seasons, they trudged into the offseason pondering what might have been.

They ruined perfect seasons for Nebraska and Virginia Tech to ascend the throne. They bowed to Florida, Tennessee, and Oklahoma with a national championship trophy on-site for presentation.

There are extenuating circumstances in every victory and every defeat: an untimely injury, a questionable penalty, a combination of events outside one's control. So out there, somewhere, there undoubtedly are FSU fans who mourn championships lost even more than they celebrate those won.

They bemoan a Texas upset of Nebraska in the 1996 Big Twelve championship game that forced the Seminoles into a Sugar Bowl

On FSU's first play, and in Travis Minor's first start, the freshman tailback took a pitchout around right end and scooted 87 yards to a touchdown and a 7–0 lead. The game was 24 seconds old. Quarterback Thad Busby passed 38 yards to Peter Warrick for a 14–0 advantage on FSU's next possession. Just two and rematch with Florida and Heisman-winning quarterback Danny Wuerffel after that 24–21 FSU survival in Tallahassee. They wonder how Tennessee would have fared against a 1998 FSU team quarterbacked by Chris Weinke rather than Marcus Outzen, who was making his third and final career start substituting for the injured Weinke in the Fiesta Bowl. They irrationally perceive missing wide receiver Marvin Minnis, an academic casualty before the 2000 team's Orange Bowl showdown with Oklahoma, as the reason an offense that averaged more than 42 points through an 11–1 regular season failed to produce a point in a 13–2 loss.

The fact is, Florida's only loss in 1996 came on that windblown November afternoon in Tallahassee, and Tennessee and Oklahoma completed perfect seasons with their victories over the Seminoles. Sometimes the other team is just better. What's the shame?

The glory of FSU football is how Bowden's teams remained factors in the national championship chase year after year after year. The NCAA football record book lists games in which the Associated Press's number one–ranked team played number two. Between November 16, 1991, and January 4, 2000, there were eight. FSU played in six of those.

FSU became accustomed to the hoopla that came with a national spotlight. As Bowden once joked, "We're living in 5000 A.D., we've had so many games of the century."

a half minutes later, receiver E. G. Green collaborated with Busby on a 74-yard touchdown play.

Six minutes and 16 seconds had elapsed. FSU had snapped the ball 5 times, scored 3 touchdowns, and led 21–0, muting a crowd that had arrived in a raucous, partying mood.

That initial twenty-nine-game conference winning streak after FSU opted to join the ACC instead of the Southeastern Conference, however, might have been snuffed at five, had Charlie Ward not rallied the Seminoles to that 29–24 victory over Georgia Tech in 1992.

That, too, fits among the great games but may rank higher than many others based on the fact that Bowden and offensive coaches Mark Richt and Brad Scott adapted to a shotgun attack that bore Ward's stamp and eventually filled the missing jewel in FSU's crown.

To refresh memories, Scott Sisson's chip-shot field goal two minutes into the fourth quarter padded the Yellow Jackets' lead to 21–7, and nothing that had happened in the first three quarters suggested that FSU still had a pulse. Bowden even benched Ward for one series midway through the third quarter after his interception left Georgia Tech with just 10 yards for the touchdown that built the Jackets' lead to 18–7. But at 21–7 Bowden made the call that not only reversed fortunes in the game but salvaged a season and altered history. He went to the fast break.

Ward proceeded to pass or run on every play except a 1-yard touchdown plunge by fullback William Floyd in touchdown drives covering 80 yards in 11 plays, 80 yards in 10 plays, and, after a successful on-side kick, 40 yards in 6 plays. In those three drives, Ward accounted for 137 yards passing and 67 rushing, the math skewed by a 5-yard penalty against the Seminoles. His 17-yard pass to Kez McCorvey on a fourth-down-and-five play with less than two minutes remaining not only snatched victory from the jaws of defeat but also laid groundwork for the sixteen victories in his final seventeen starts.

Back to the subject of trick plays, puntrooskie reduces all the rest to pretenders: the fake field goals that worked at Ohio State and at Michigan, the "fumblerooskie" that backfired and dealt FSU a 1990 loss at Auburn, and the throwback bounce pass on the kickoff-return touchdown at Miami in 1986. The fact is, once Bowden's program hit its championship-contending stride in the 1987 season robbed of perfection by a failed two-point pass, the Seminoles rarely needed subterfuge to conquer. But when they did need it that 1988 afternoon at Clemson, they unveiled the trick play against which all others are measured—and found lacking.

# Best of the Best

Marvin Jones, an assassin in pads, had played only four games as a freshman before Florida State defensive coordinator Mickey Andrews assessed his performance in terms that left no gray area about rarified ability. "He's every bit as talented at his position as Deion Sanders was at his," Andrews said after watching Marvelous Marvin punish Virginia Tech ball carriers with 21 tackles. "And I'll guarantee you he's a lot further along as a freshman."

By the time Jones departed a year early for the NFL, he had become FSU's third two-time consensus All-American and swept the 1992 Butkus Award as the nation's top linebacker and the Lombardi Award that goes to a linebacker or defensive lineman. But no award defined Jones's football disposition better than a poster documenting a whiplash hit Jones put on a University of Miami back his junior season. Jones left welts and bruises as evidence that he had paid a jolting visit.

"Maybe as good a hitter as has ever been through here," Andrews said. "He had the best knack of uncoiling and punishing a blocker or a ballcarrier." Andrews weighed whether he wanted to elaborate on the image, and then added almost furtively, "You don't brag about this, but I think one year he broke three quarterbacks' jaws."

Jones, who had been a USA Today and Parade All-American at Miami Northwestern High, impishly said during his freshman season that it took him until "the first day in pads" to convince FSU coaches his high school credentials weren't embellished.

Number 55 became a player upon whom eyes riveted once an FSU opponent snapped the ball. Seeing Jones drive into a ballcarrier when both had a full head of steam was like watching meteors collide. If Jones was moving forward, he continued moving forward.

I once asked him to describe what it felt like to hit someone as jarringly as he did regularly. "It has something to do with physics," he replied. "When I really focus in on a person, really

*Linebacker Marvin Jones, zoning in on a ballcarrier, had to rank as one of the most fearsome sights in college football in the early 1990s.*

concentrate on that specific object, I don't actually see him. I look *through* him." Then he'd drive through him as if he were trying to get to the other side.

"When I know I've made a good hit is when I collide with you and my mind looks . . . I mean, like lightning has struck and my mind just goes blank. I don't actually feel the hit. I don't hear anything. It's like playing tape with sound and [the sound] just stops . . . and gradually it comes back.

"I love it. I love contact."

A long-time NFL scout once told me that two collegians had received the highest grade he had awarded. One was North Carolina linebacker Lawrence Taylor, later elected to the NFL Hall of Fame. The other was Marvin Jones, whose own twelve-year NFL career was productive but diminished by knee injuries.

Headliners like Jones and Sanders serve as reminders of what an extraordinary succession of superstar careers played out before my eyes. It also prompted this for-fun exercise of assembling a Florida State all-star but not all-time lineup, since this one's confined to those about whom I wrote over the two decades from 1981 through 2000.

Distinguishing the best of the best, naturally, is a task designed to prod memories but inevitably to stir dissent as well. At many positions, the mission becomes one of splitting hairs. How can there be a wrong answer to the question of which of two Heisman Trophy winners, Charlie Ward or Chris Weinke, should be first-team quarterback in this mythical, even mystical, exercise?

But nothing ventured, nothing to argue about. So here they are, position by position.

# Quarterback Charlie Ward

The mercurial 1993 Heisman winner gets the nod over 1999 Heisman recipient Weinke primarily because an explosive concept of offense evolved from Ward's surreal blend of passing and running skills and his poise. Ward appeared to have eyes in the front, back, and sides of his head.

I wrote once that if the bottoms of his shoes bore wet paint, most defenders would be using turpentine to remove it from their fingertips at game's end. Ward constantly was stepping out of danger just when you thought he was going to get walloped. Weinke finished with better numbers as a passer, but Ward thrilled observers both passing and running.

# Running Backs Greg Allen and Warrick Dunn

Allen, from tiny Milton, Florida, ranks second only to Dunn in career rushing yards with 3,769. He led the Seminoles in three of his four seasons from 1981 through 1984.

On the first carry of his first career start, he swept around end for 66 yards at Louisiana State and finished with 202 yards on 31 carries in a 38–14 rout. In his second start, he rushed for an FSU-record 322 yards on 32 carries in a 56–31 romp past Western Carolina. He also scored on a 95-yard kickoff return, and his 417 all-purpose yards established an NCAA Division 1-A single-game record, since eclipsed. That elevated expectations for the balance of Allen's career, but as a sophomore, he carried for 20 of his 44 career rushing touchdowns, both FSU records.

Guard Jamie Dukes once said of the sculpted Allen: "I've seen Greg literally jump over a guy's head. There's not an ounce of fat on [Allen's rock-hard legs]. I'll bet if they checked, there would be point-zero-zero fat. Greg is just cut-to-the-max muscle."

This by no means is a mathematical exercise, but Dunn surpassed Allen to become FSU's all-time leading rusher with 3,959 yards from 1993 through 1996. Stunningly, during a record-breaking junior season in which he carried for 1,242 yards, Dunn's average *per carry* didn't slip beneath 10 yards until the seventh game, and he finished with a 7.5-yard average for the season.

I remember a spectacular photo in the *Tallahassee Democrat* showing Dunn in midhurdle over lunging defenders with his head pointed forward but his eyes shifted to his right anticipating the first move once he landed.

"If he weighed 215 pounds," Bobby Bowden once said, "he'd be illegal." Both as a Seminole and later as an NFL standout, Dunn defied the perception that he couldn't operate as a heavy-duty back because of his 180-pound frame. But, he playfully rationalized, "That just shows you that a coach cares not just about a football game. He's trying not to get me killed." The humor disappeared when he added, "It's up to me to prove [Bowden] wrong and show that I can take it." He showed Bowden. He since has proved his durability to NFL coaches as well.

# Wide Receivers Peter Warrick and Lawrence Dawsey

Were this an all-time team, 1960s stars Fred Biletnikoff and Ron Sellers, the first two Seminoles to have their numbers retired, would be locks. But that diminishes in no way the exploits of Warrick and Dawsey. Warrick ranks second to Sellers in FSU career receptions and yards and number one in touchdown catches with 31. Dawsey not only ran precise routes and caught anything within reach but also exhibited a toughness rare in a "skill" player.

Few players have ever been blessed with the array of moves with which Warrick could make defenders look silly. Rival cornerbacks often relished a matchup against Warrick as a test of their manhood . . . until he staggered them with a stop-and-go move, pogo'd to pluck a potential interception off their fingertips, or showed them the back of his number 9 jersey as he drew away like a speeding car's disappearing taillights.

In late 1998 offensive coordinator Mark Richt said, "I don't know if there's anybody in this program since I've been here [1990] that can be as *electric* as Pete." It was not a qualification but a compliment that he added Charlie Ward and Warrick Dunn to the conversation.

Dawsey did not have Warrick's moves, his speed, or his flair. But *nobody* who has lined up at wide receiver for Florida State had Dawsey's physical and mental toughness. Blocking is no receiver's first love. But Dawsey excelled at it. "I have never seen a receiver hit people like Dawsey hits them," wide receivers coach John Eason said.

But that was just part of the package. He made the clutch plays in the tough games. He had six 100-yard receiving games during his All-America season as a senior in 1990, but I vividly recall two performances: one in victory, one in defeat.

In FSU's first square-off against a Steve Spurrier–coached

Florida team, Dawsey's escape on a 76-yard touchdown play launched the Seminoles toward a 45–30 victory, and a 71-yard hookup with Casey Weldon secured it. Even more impressive was a 13-catch, 160-yard performance at Miami. The Seminoles lost, 31–22, but Dawsey was indomitable. In a *Miami Herald* photo the next day, he was shown soaring above a throng of defenders, his hips almost at head-level, one arm extended toward the sky for a one-handed catch.

## Center Clay Shiver and Guards Jamie Dukes and Jason Whitaker

Through much of the 1970s, I served as beat reporter or backup covering the Miami Dolphins and a trio of offensive linemen without peer. Center Jim Langer and guard Larry Little are in the NFL Hall of Fame. Guard Bob Kuechenberg should be and probably isn't only because voting pro football writers prefer to spread the laurels. It was either Kuechenberg or line coach Monte Clark who called offensive linemen mushrooms because they were put in a dark corner and fed manure. But the special ones emerge into the light of stardom over time.

Because the eye follows the football, linemen's exploits become camouflaged by the massive line-of-scrimmage scrums that represent, on every play, a test of strength, will, and pain tolerance. But center Clay Shiver (1995) and guards Jamie Dukes (1985) and Jason Whitaker (1999) all warranted the All-America honors that came their way. Parallels to Langer, Little, and Kuechenberg in skill, style, and demeanor are loose, given the pro-vs.-college level of competition, but not without validity.

Shiver, like Langer, was a lunch-pail guy who set an example not only with an exceptional work ethic but also with a measured, low-key leadership. His perspective on life flowed into his football. Bowden relied on him to counsel other players. "I believe it's the older players' responsibility to look after the younger guys," Shiver once said. "They know a lot about football, but they don't know a lot about FSU football yet."

Bowden didn't have to work hard to recruit the *Parade* All-American from Tifton, Georgia. Shiver's older brother Stan preceded Clay to FSU and left a mark as arguably the hardest-hitting safety to wear Seminole colors.

The comparison between Dukes and Little is generated mostly by the terror both instilled in overmatched defensive backs when they exploded from their stance to pull and lead toss-sweeps. Dukes, who started every one of his forty-eight games at FSU, had a quick first step but gained momentum like a refrigerator on wheels going downhill.

Equating Whitaker to Kuechenberg, the first attributes that leap to mind are sense of humor and self-deprecating wit. Kuechenberg's came naturally. Before his father became an Indiana farmer, he was a human cannonball in a circus. Whitaker's cleverness peaked when he was poking fun at himself.

Before FSU capped its 1998 regular season with a 23–12 upset of Florida, Whitaker spoke of his embarrassment against the Gators the year before. "I've never had anyone pick me up, twirl me around on his finger, and throw me away like that," he quipped, exaggerating outrageously but only to admit how badly he had been outplayed by Florida defensive tackle Ed Chester. "[Announcers] called me a blocking sled for Ed Chester on national television."

Whitaker was no man's blocking sled during a 1999 perfect season in which he became FSU's first consensus All-America offensive lineman since Shiver.

## Offensive Tackles Walter Jones and Tra Thomas and Tight End Pat Carter

I have a confession. If an FSU coach told me today that Walter Jones's performance in 1996 or Tra Thomas's in 1997 was solid but not exceptional, I'd believe him. To pretend to be an expert on offensive tackle play without watching videotape until your eyeballs become square or sharing a practice field with them week after week would be presumptuous. But I recall sitting with receivers E. G. Green and Andre Cooper in the lobby of a Miami hotel the week before the Orange Bowl that capped the 1995 season and having both predict that Jones, redshirted that year after transferring from a junior college, would be the best offensive lineman ever to play at FSU.

Jones lined up for FSU for only one season. But he made such an impression as a junior in 1996 that he declared his eligibility for the NFL draft and became the sixth player selected. Anyone who watched Seattle playoff victories on the path to the 2006 Super Bowl heard one analyst after another describe Jones not just as the best tackle in pro ranks but as the best offensive lineman as well.

Tra Thomas, a first-round draft choice of the Philadelphia Eagles in 1997, also has earned Pro Bowl recognition. Thomas, incidentally, backed up Jones in 1996 before starting two games on the opposite side when tackle Todd Fordham moved inside to replace injured guard Chad Bates. Fordham also has established himself in the pros. How's that for a trio on one college roster.

Pat Carter, like most FSU tight ends, made a greater impression as a blocker than as a pass catcher in Tallahassee. For that reason, receiving statistics became irrelevant in attempting to choose from among Carter, Reggie Johnson, and Lonnie Johnson. All three became second-round NFL draft picks. All three had extensive pro careers. But Carter sticks out in my mind because of his contributions to a 1987 team that positioned FSU to contend for the national championship that year and in the next thirteen, too.

## Placekicker Sebastian Janikowski

No contest. Watching the guy kick off was practically worth the price of admission. Officials usually could have saved time by simply putting the ball on the opponent's 20-yard line. Touchbacks were the norm, not the exception. But the Polish thunderfoot possessed accuracy to match his strength. The first two-time winner of the Groza Award signifying college football's best placekicker, Janikowski made 66 of 83 career field-goal attempts, five of the successes ranging from 52 to 56 yards.

Coaches, sports information directors, and media members voted for the Walter Camp Foundation's all-century team after the 1999 season. Janikowski was one of four placekickers and one of three Seminoles, joining wide receiver Fred Biletnikoff and cornerback Deion Sanders.

Janikowski joked before he entered the 2000 NFL draft with

*Thunderfoot Sebastian Janikowski racked up 66 field goals in 83 attempts during his career at FSU.*

a year of eligibility remaining that he would return to FSU for his senior season if Coach Bowden would let him play linebacker. Bowden, dead serious about Janikowski's rugged makeup, said Janikowski would have been a good one.

## Defensive Ends Peter Boulware and Reinard Wilson

First, necessarily, a word about those not selected: Cast aside here are a Lombardi Award winner (Jamal Reynolds, 2000), at least temporarily a third consensus All-American (Andre Wadsworth, 1997), and a two-time All-American (Derrick Alexander, 1993 and 1994). If FSU hadn't already become known as Cornerback U. for a succession of All-Americans beginning with Deion Sanders, it would have warranted a Defensive-End U. tag in the 1990s.

But Boulware and Wilson so dominated in their lockstep careers, each in his own distinctive way, that proclaiming them the best of the best shouldn't provoke heated debate. Boulware was incredibly quick, Wilson incredibly strong, and it simply was too much to ask of an offense to double-team both.

Defensive coordinator Mickey Andrews shook his head in wonder one time during that 1996 season as he observed, "Here's Reinard, chasing and breaking Ron Simmons's school record for career sacks. And now he's chasing it again."

That's because Boulware, in the midst of sacking quarterbacks a single-season-record 19 times that year, had caught and exceeded Wilson's total. Wilson eventually reclaimed the record with 35½ sacks to Boulware's 34. In 1996 alone they combined for 32½, and Andrews marveled recently, "We went that one year where we did not run a single blitz. A four-man rush is all we ever had." In that same conversation, without playing one off against the other, Andrews also said, "Reinard might have been, pound for pound, as good a player as we've ever had. He was relentless and just ungodly strong for his size."

Though a modest 255 pounds, not that large for a defensive end, Wilson shoved 300-pound offensive tackles around as if they were on roller skates. Longtime defensive ends coach Jim Gladden once comically described a Wilson sack against Maryland this way: "Reinard took that tackle and had both the guy's feet off the ground and just wadded him up with the quarterback. He ended up with the quarterback under the tackle in a pile, and Reinard's sorting through it for the football like a dog hunting a bone."

Leave it to Wilson to best reflect on one of Boulware's greatest attributes, a fierce and fiery temperament that contrasted greatly with Wilson's country-boy calm. Boulware played with a maniacal zeal that belied his sharp intellect and congeniality off the field. Wilson tolerated blockers who resorted to holding because he understood their plight. Asked what he'd do if he were a tackle assigned to block Reinard Wilson, Reinard admitted, "I'd hold every play . . . The worst thing that can happen is a 10-yard penalty. The referee may call it one time. But most games they haven't called any."

Boulware, by contrast, would turn his fury on officials who were blind to the fact a tackle had just literally tackled him rather than let him punish a quarterback. The amused Wilson tattled, "You've never heard [Boulware] use the words he says to referees. I don't think he knows he's saying some stuff he says. We tell him the next day, and he says, 'I didn't say that.' And everybody says, 'You did, Pete. You said it.'"

## Defensive Tackles Corey Simon, Odell Haggins, and Andre Wadsworth

Okay, you caught me. That's one too many. But two disclaimers:

First, I never covered FSU nose tackle *nonpareil* Ron Simmons, who left to make his fortune as a professional wrestler after the 1980 season, one year before I was assigned the beat. And second, after singling out Simon, I decided not to choose between Haggins, an inspirational player in the late 1980s who joined Bowden's coaching staff in 1993, and Wadsworth, who benefited from Haggins's tutelage as a nose tackle in 1996 before he was moved outside in 1997 and earned All-America honors as an end.

Beyond their football exploits Haggins, Wadsworth, and Simon all exhibited qualities that could impress you before they ever put on shoulder pads and a helmet: Haggins with his energy and enthusiastic storm-the-fort leadership, Wadsworth with his intelligence, and Simon with all of the above.

Aside from an agate line of type citing his 8 sacks in 1987, no numerical measure exists in FSU's record book to underscore Haggins's role in the Seminoles' emergence as a football super-power. Indeed, though the achievements of Wadsworth and Simon are documented in a press-guide section on consensus All-Americans, my lingering memories of both extend beyond the playing field.

Wadsworth, who played at tiny Florida Christian High in Miami, arrived at FSU as a walk-on. Chuck Amato, then FSU's assistant head coach and now North Carolina State's head coach, used to laugh when complimented for persuading Wadsworth to enroll. "It's embarrassing now to think we didn't offer Andre a scholarship right away," he'd counter. But Wadsworth, the third player selected in the 1998 NFL draft, also questioned whether his small-school experience would prepare him for major college competition. He was in New Orleans preparing for FSU's 31–14 Sugar Bowl domination of Ohio State in his final collegiate game

# Super Players, Better Citizens

Betty Dunn Smothers, a single mother, worked as a police officer in Baton Rouge, Louisiana, to support her six children. She never achieved the financial security that would have permitted her to purchase her own home.

It has been in tribute to his mother, who was shot and killed on duty in January 1993, that former Florida State University standout Warrick Dunn has established a charitable foundation whose primary mission is the Homes for the Holidays program that enables economically disadvantaged single mothers to own their own homes.

Dunn not only provides down payments on the purchases but also works with area sponsors to furnish the homes. The program has benefited more than fifty families, not only in Baton Rouge but in Tampa, Florida, and Atlanta, Georgia, too, the cities where Dunn has achieved NFL stardom.

Few sports figures have ever impressed me more than the soft-spoken Dunn. He had become the man of the house even before his mother's death. But that tragedy forced adulthood on a seventeen-year-old who became a head of household. I always felt that his decision to remain at FSU for his senior season rather than make an early entry into the NFL was an attempt to salvage what was left of a compressed, suppressed youth.

I'll never forget a conversation before his senior season, in which Dunn, addressing how he counseled his younger brothers and sisters, said: "The kids in the nineties are so much different than when I was growing up." He was twenty-one years old. This was pointed out to him. "Probably, mind-wise, I feel old," he responded. "But in spirit I want to be like a teenager again."

The NFL recognized Dunn's marvelous deeds by awarding him its Walter Payton Man of the Year Award in 2005. He became the second Seminole to be honored with the league's prestigious recognition of extraordinary community service.

Derrick Brooks, Tampa Bay linebacker and perennial all-pro, shared the Man of the Year Award in 2000. He annually organizes and serves as a guide on educational excursions for youngsters in the Tampa Bay area.

when he spoke of a letter he received while home for Christmas.

Puzzled at first, he quickly recognized the handwriting and the content. "I was in an advanced-placement English class my senior year in high school," he said, "and the teacher had us write where we wanted to be in five years. After those five years, they mail [the essay] back to you." He chuckled. He had written that he possibly had suited up for the final time for any sport. To the great benefit of FSU, he hadn't.

Simon, a Pro Bowl invitee for the Philadelphia Eagles in 2003 and an invaluable addition to the Indianapolis Colts' defense in 2005, always impressed me as a greater inspiration off the field than a destructive force on it. Rob Wilson, FSU's sports information director, attended Lombardi Award ceremonies after the 1999 season and spoke of the impact Simon's tribute to cancer-stricken children in attendance had on the audience.

"When Corey finished [speaking], there wasn't a sound in the room," Wilson said. "Everybody was fighting back tears. The emcee, the radio announcer for the Dallas Cowboys, stood up at the microphone and started to talk. But he said, 'I've got to have a minute to compose myself,' and he backed off. It was that dramatic."

Simon spoke of that night as an experience "everybody needs to go through, especially anybody in the athletic arena . . . To see those kids, who have to battle for their lives every day, to whom it's a blessing to be able to wake up and enjoy another day . . . that was definitely a life-changing experience for me."

I'll add the asterisk that Simon embodied a mature and admirable perspective on life before he ever wore number 53 into a game for FSU.

# Linebackers Paul McGowan, Marvin Jones, and Derrick Brooks

Paul McGowan, much greater than the sum of his physical parts, had suspect size and speed. But the heart with which he attacked the game at full throttle was beyond compare. The inaugural winner of the Butkus Award in 1987, McGowan narrowly out-pointed a player of similar size and kindred spirit, Ohio State's Chris Spielman.

Jones, by contrast, was built to pro specifications and flaunted pro form from the moment he stepped onto FSU's campus. Not only did he collect the Butkus and Lombardi awards before departing a year early to become the fourth player selected in the 1993 NFL draft, he also finished fourth in Heisman Trophy bal-loting and arguably could be seen as more deserving than the three who outpolled him, including the recipient, Miami quar-terback Gino Torretta.

Brooks didn't win the Butkus Award, but he finished runner-up to Nebraska's Trev Alberts in 1993. Brooks, the big-play cata-lyst on a defense that posted four shutouts and limited two other rivals to 7 or fewer points, literally outscored FSU's first five vic-tims combined, 18–14, with touchdowns on fumble or intercep-tion returns. Brooks has become a perennial Pro Bowler at Tampa Bay. No one, Andrews said, had greater awareness of what was happening on the field. "He could see not only the move-ment of the ball but movement of the blockers. It was uncanny."

# Cornerbacks Deion Sanders and Terrell Buckley

It's still mind-blowing to me that during the 2005 NFL season, both Deion Sanders and Terrell Buckley—who last played at FSU in 1988 and 1991, respectively—still were earning NFL paychecks.

Andrews recalled that Sanders played quarterback in a wishbone attack in high school, had the option at FSU to line up at either wide receiver or cornerback, and chose to play defense because "he saw more good receivers on our team than defensive backs."

# Safeties LeRoy Butler and Derrick Gibson

True, LeRoy Butler, forever identified as the lead actor in puntrookie, earned All-America honors as a cornerback in 1989. But he starred at safety before coaches filled a desperate need by shifting him to the corner for his senior season. He also enjoyed an illustrious pro career in Green Bay as a safety.

Andrews recalled force-feeding Butler cornerback technique through the 1989 spring drills and into fall practice and Butler struggling mightily to pick it up. A stickler for detail, Andrews said he learned a valuable lesson in the process. "I was determined LeRoy was going to play corner the way I wanted him to play it, and he couldn't do it my way. I finally said, 'OK LeRoy, there are some liabilities your way, but we're not going to make you into a robot.'"

There was a direct correlation between Butler achieving comfort at the position and the 1989 Seminoles rebounding from losses in which they gave up 30 points to Brett Favre and Southern Mississippi and then 34 to Clemson before a subsequent string of ten victories in which rivals averaged 13.5 points.

A lively debate could accompany designation of the second safety on this honor roll. You could argue for:

- Stan Shiver, a hitter in the mold of, say, longtime pro John Lynch
- Devin Bush, the Miami native who sealed that ghost-busting 28–10 victory over the Hurricanes with his interception and touchdown return midway through the 1993 national championship season and who became a first-round NFL draftee in 1995
- Dexter Jackson, an efficient Seminole who became the second ex-Seminole to win Most Valuable Player honors in a Super Bowl. He intercepted two Rich Gannon passes in Tampa Bay's 48–21 rout of Oakland (Trivia: Fred Biletnikoff was the first, for the Oakland Raiders.)

But on the entire body of evidence, Gibson best combined ball-hawking instincts (7 career interceptions) with run-support muscle (214 career tackles). If you need more to tilt the scales, consider that in all three seasons in which Gibson started at strong safety, the Seminoles played in the national-championship game.

# Punter Rohn Stark

Stark, whose punts threatened low-hanging clouds, vaulted from a four-year career at FSU into a fifteen-year career in the NFL, mostly for the Indianapolis Colts. I covered only his senior season, in 1981. But I saw him average an FSU single-game record 54.8 yards against Florida to help him establish an FSU-record 46.0 yards for a single season.

Thus endeth the exercise and starteth the debate.

# About the Author

**Gary Long,** an Indiana University graduate, began a thirty-six-year career with the *Miami Herald* in September 1965 after two years as a lieutenant in the U.S. Army and ten months working for the *Decatur* (Illinois) *Herald & Review*. His versatility led to a wide assortment of assignments. He covered more than a dozen Super Bowls, two Olympic Games (1984, 1996), seven NCAA basketball Final Fours, four Kentucky Derbys, more than twenty Indianapolis 500s, upwards of thirty Daytona 500s, and the odd Major League Baseball playoff game, tennis match, and boxing bout.

He interviewed and wrote about Chris Evert when she was ten years old, Sugar Ray Leonard when he was nineteen, Richard Petty when he was thirty-two, and Don Shula when he was thirty-nine. Favorite interview subjects have ranged from Muhammad Ali to Mario Andretti, from Akeem Olajuwon to D. Wayne Lukas, from Jimmy Valvano to Bobby Allison. Oh, yeah, and a couple of race drivers named Paul Newman and Gene Hackman.

But the name that has popped up in Long's body of work more than any other has to be Bobby Bowden's. The author covered the Florida State football beat for the *Herald* from 1981 through his (semi-) retirement in mid-2001. The Seminoles' unmatched string of fourteen consecutive seasons marked by double-digit victories and a postbowls ranking between number one and number five provided the events and memories that compose the bulk of this book.